# All Color World of
# HORSES

# All Color World of
# HORSES

## Peter Churchill

octopus

# Contents

Jacket: A Palomino mare and foal.
Endpapers: The Halflinger breed originated
from the Austrian Tyrol.
Title page: Semi-wild horses show the herd
characteristics held by their ancestors before Man
domesticated the species.
This page: A Welsh Mountain pony.

First published 1978 by Octopus Books Limited
59 Grosvenor Street, London W1

© 1978 Octopus Books Limited
ISBN 0 7064 0747 4
Produced by Mandarin Publishers Limited
22a Westlands Road, Quarry Bay, Hong Kong.

Printed in Hong Kong

# Introduction

In this book I have set out to trace the milestones of the horse's history, the origins of some of the world's native breeds and man-made breeds and the role of the horse in our leisure, sport, and working lives.

We start with some background on the evolution of the horse before meeting many of the varied breeds that exist around the world. From the tiny and delightful Shetland pony through to the sleek and glamourous thoroughbred and Arab then on to the practical and still serving working breeds such as the Shire, Percheron, Breton and the active little Haflinger pony. From breeds we go to the horse at work. This is an area in which the horse has served Man in countless valuable ways but my favourite story of a working horse is that of the American Morgan horse. There are several versions of the fascinating tale of that brilliant little stallion 'Justin Morgan'. His origins and daily life, as in many legends, differ in each version but there is no shadow of doubt that 'Justin' created one of the finest general purpose horses in continental America.

After a short look at the Horse at Play and some of the man-created vices that the domesticated horse can suffer from, we go on to pageantry and the vast world of equestrian sports. Horse-racing is one of the leading spectator sports in the world but international show jumping, eventing, trail riding and the rodeo are also capturing bigger audiences with each new season.

The horse has always appealed to Man's imagination and emotions and in Horses in Art we look at some of the great artists of the equestrian world before the coming of the all-seeing camera. In Care of the Horse the book covers the principles governing the care of them. But it is a never ending subject which as many of the old horsemasters used to say of it . . .

'The day you know it all is the day you get it wrong'.

In the latter part of this century the horse and pony have experienced a great revival in their popularity and use perhaps never equalled in their long and fascinating history. Pony and Riding Clubs are thriving almost everywhere. Horse Shows report record crowds and millions of telespectators see the big championships or top races almost as they happen anywhere in the world.

Beyond that are the countless enthusiasts who ride at weekends or spend long, pleasurable hours helping their youngsters to get their mounts ready for the local rally or show. All are very much part of the colourful world of horses.

Left: The sparring action of two young colts is a foretaste of the way in which grown stallions would battle for the control of a herd of mares if they were wild.
Right: A group of riders clearly showing the pleasure that can be gained from the sport.

# Horses around the world

We know very little of the true origins of the horse for archaeologists are still finding new evidence that either up-dates or pre-dates theories that have been held for centuries. But from the study of fossils and remains found in America, south-east England and western Europe, we do have considerable evidence that points to *Eohippus* and *Orohippus* who lived during the Eocene period, as being the earliest members of the horse family. These strong-looking little creatures, some 38 cms (10.5 ins) in height, lived in small herds. *Eohippus* seems to have been the more common species, roaming areas that are now America, England and Europe. While *Orohippus* does not seem to have travelled beyond North America.

By the Oligocene period, some 40 to 25 million years before our time, *Epihippus* and *Mesohippus* had evolved. These creatures lived in forests in central, eastern and southern America. The environment gradually altered during the centuries and the thick forests began to give way to open woodland and plains. The herds gradually moved out onto the plains in their constant search for food and safety. It was here that the real horse began to develop and find his true home in the wide open spaces of the prairies.

**Left: The Iceland pony was introduced into the region by Norwegians during the 9th century.**
**Below: The Shetland pony, smallest of the British native breeds, is popular as a child's first pony.**

Now evolution of the horse became more rapid and the equine's body began to develop more strength and depth. The legs grew longer bringing the height up to 51 to 71 cms (20 ins to 28 ins), and the form of his feet changed to three toes and harder pads. It is interesting that the embryo of the modern horse at six weeks still has this three-toed conformation. The early primitives were now taking on a definite horse-like look and with danger ever-present, their alertness and speed were becoming an effective means of defence.

During the Miocene period, some 25 to 10 million years ago, the world faced part of its most dramatic and violent geophysical changes. Forests and vegetation became more nutritious and developed definite regions. Likewise, the animal kingdom responded to these changes by evolving more diverse species which began moving across the land masses. The herds of small horse-like creatures now began their long trek over the Bering Straits to Europe.

Two quite definite horse-families now began to establish themselves: the *Parahippus* and *Merychippus*, both standing at nearly one metre (3 ft). They settled on the eastern and western seaboards of North America, but many wandered as far as the Rockies in the north and the Panama canal in the south. The *Merychippus* is the more interesting of the two for he developed at a faster rate, and his strong straight back and erect mane made him the more similar to a modern horse.

Man had still not appeared on Earth when the herds of horses made their most dramatic move during the Pliocene period, some 10 to 1 million years before our time. Severe cold was to drive them over the Bering Straits into the new land-mass that is now Europe and Asia. It was mainly the *Hipparion* that made this journey which extended as far as the Far East and North Africa. While the *Pliohippus* stayed on in North America until moving south in search of warmth and food, a journey that was eventually to lead him to extinction.

Some experts say that the *Hipparion* was the ancestor of the zebra and wild ass, others think that he was the forefather of the true horse. Regardless of which of these theories is correct, we now have a very horse-like creature with one toe settled and thriving in Europe. So now in Europe, Northern Spain, mid-Asia and the Middle East roamed herds of grass-eating solipeds, half-pony half-ass. Here was the creature that was to help Man feed his family, travel and trade with his neighbours, and also create and destroy great civilizations and empires, a partnership destined to endure through the centuries.

The environment had now settled to the familiar pattern of seas, mountains, plains, forests, deserts, rivers and plateaus. Man either wandered in small groups or half-settled in cave dwelling communities. The family of the horse, like other creatures, also adapted its development to the environment in which it lived. In the north *Equus giganteus* arrived; a heavy ungainly creature that was probably the forefather of the great horse of Europe. In Spain, North Africa and the Middle East, the *Equus hemionus*, the onager or wild ass, was one of the earliest members of the horse family to be hunted and domesticated by Man. In Africa, existed the *Equus hippotigris* or Zebra and the *Equus caballus przewalskii* or Mongolian Wild Horse, a small half-pony, half-donkey creature.

*Equus caballus przewalskii* was discovered some 90 years ago by the Russian explorer Professor M. M. Przewalski in the depths of Mongolia. They are believed to be one of about four species that survived the Ice-age. They are small, dun or bay ponies standing 12.2 hh to 14.2 hh (124 cms to 144 cms) in height but their erect manes and dorsal stripe suggest

**Left: The Mongolian Wild Horse, 'Equus caballus przewalskii', is thought to be the last remaining wild strain and one of the ancestors of the modern horse. The Survival Service Committee is actively trying to prevent the extinction of these unique horses. The governments of the USSR, China and Mongolia have made them a protected breed.**
**Right: Two young New Forest ponies wait to be auctioned at the annual Pony Sales held at Beaulieu Road, on the edge of the forest. The New Forest pony is one of the nine breeds that make up the Mountain and Moorland group of British native ponies.**

the influence of the Wild Ass somewhere in their breeding line. So whether this attractive, stocky creature is the father of our modern horse is, to say the least, questionable. It is much more likely that he is some sort of cousin to the native ponies and cobs we see around the world today.

Where then was that pre-history 'heavenly horse' with the flying hooves said to be worth a Chinese Emperor's ransom? The truth is that we really do not know yet. But certainly the Przewalski pony and the Tarpan, another species from the Ice-Age, are very close in looks and type to the cave drawings that have been found in central France and Spain.

Before Man settled and created townships, one of the earliest settlements was the Neolithic town of Catal Hüyük in Anatolia. We know from the study of remains that there were two main types of horse, the Northern Horse and the Southern Horse. These two groups which divided naturally into 'cold-blooded' and 'warm-blooded' breeds, certainly seem to have been the main sources for the many different types of horses and ponies that exist to-day.

The classifications, 'cold-blood' and 'warm-blood', have nothing to do with the blood or body temperature but more to do with temperament and type. The cold-blooded group, which originated from the Northern horse, had to cope with often severe and variable climatic conditions so nature equipped them with more layers of skin. This thicker skin protected the veins and made the horse's or pony's body less sensitive to high winds, gorse or tree branches and forest vegetation. For example, the Forest or Diluvial horse, another breed that survived the Ice-Ages, was a northern cold-blooded horse that lived in Scandanavia and north-west Germany probably some 10,000 years ago or more. Lush pastures covering much of Europe encouraged these passive creatures to develop enormous bodies and great muscular strength. These were ancestors of the cold-blooded heavy horses that are bred in France, Scandinavia, Holland, England and Germany today.

The warm-blooded type, originating from the southern horse, lived in regions with more even climates, with less extremes between the seasons. The warm-blooded type had less layers of skin to aid circulation and to make life more comfortable for him through long, hot, dry summers. This thinner skin made these horses more sensitive to touch. An example of this type is the Thoroughbred and Arab strains of horse which have to be ridden with more care and delicacy.

Those early days of evolution and pre-history, have left the world with a large and fascinating range of horses and ponies. Many are indigenous to their present lands while others have been in-bred or cross-bred with breeds of other countries. Some breeds migrated with conquering armies while others were transported by Man to suit his needs.

One of the most popular and best loved of the pony breeds is the Shetland pony. The Shetland Islands, which lie off the coast of Northern Scotland, are the home of these tough, hardy ponies. From the remains found on the Islands it seems that they were domesticated as far back as the Bronze Age, some 2500 years ago. The original ponies came to Britain just before the ice-fields melted and were of Tundra origin, standing about 13.2 hh high. During the centuries, their size became smaller and apart from the breed influence of stallions brought in by the first Norse settlers some 1000 years ago they have remained pure-bred.

Black and brown are the most common colours with chesnut and grey becoming very popular in recent years but any colour is more or less acceptable. Roan, dun and cream are now scarce although skewbald and piebald can still be found on the Islands.

As late as 1850 there were no roads on the Isles so the only means of transport was pony or boat. The Shetland pony soon made a name for himself as a dual purpose animal, capable of carrying heavy loads

or humans over rough and difficult terrain. But in Britain, around 1860 there was a big demand for ponies to work underground in the expanding coal-mines of north-east England. The Shetland was now developed for draught work and a thick, heavier type was bred. Now with mechanization this pattern of Shetland has largely disappeared.

These ponies, popular all over the world in the show ring and as childrens' first ponies, are docile, gentle and easy to train. They have a brave character and great versatility which is not relative to their size. In recent years they have become popular in Driving Scurry contests, a sort of chariot race against time where several 'gates' made of plastic cones have to be negotiated.

The Shetland pony can now be seen in many countries of the world, such as the USA, Canada and the Falkland Islands. They can adapt easily to foreign climates without any deviation from true type or size. The leading importers now are Holland, Sweden, Denmark, Belgium and France who all have their own stud books for the breed.

Perhaps Great Britain's most important contribution to the pony world is her Mountain and Moorland strains of native pony. Welsh, Shetland, Dartmoor, New Forest, Highland, Exmoor, Fell, Dales and Connemara breeds make up this group. These are all strains of ponies that can now be seen almost anywhere in the world. The smaller type of Connemara Pony, for example, is very popular in America. The Connemara is a native of western seaboard of Eire. The present stud book was opened in 1923 by the local Pony Society and the department of Agriculture. Now all stallions in Ireland have to be licensed by the government. The ideal Connemara should stand at about 13.2 hh (approximately 132 cms), is hardy, docile and tireless with good shoulders and a free, flowing action. They are ponies of great antiquity and it is thought they have more than a sprinkling of Spanish and Arab blood running through their veins due, most probably, to the merchants of Galway trading with Spain. In latter years Thoroughbred and part-Arab blood was put into the breed and one of the Thoroughbred stallions, Little Haven, when mated with a Connemara mare produced the famous little Irish international show jumper Dundrum ridden with such success by Tommy Wade in the early 1960s.

All these native breeds of the British Isles have romantic stories. There are stories of their travels, for they are now exported all over the world or of their fight for survival after the industrial revolution, when so many of them were replaced by machinery and vehicles. One such breed is the handsome and versatile Dales Pony. In the early 1950s the Dales Pony had almost disappeared but thanks to a few dedicated breeders and the arrival of a new pastime, pony trekking, the breed has come back and is as

Opposite: The fascinating Chincoteague ponies are named after the islands where they live, off the coast of Virginia and Maryland, USA. Each July, they are rounded up and made to swim to Assateague, a neighbouring island, for an annual auction sale.
Above: The Camargue horse or 'white, wild horse of the sea' lives in the Camargue, an area of swampland lying at the mouth of the Rhone in southern France. They are thought to be of very ancient origin, descended from the Solurean 'ram-headed horse', a forerunner of the modern Barb.
Below: Exmoor, a moorland and forest area crossing Devonshire and Somerset in south-western England is the home of the attractive Exmoor pony. These hardy ponies are one of the most distinctive of the British native breeds. They have 'mealy' coloured noses with very prominent wide-set eyes. The upper and lower lids are a mealy colour and are known locally as 'toad-eyes'.

Left: The gentle and courageous Welsh pony has roamed the Welsh hills since pre-history. These agile ponies are natural jumpers and because of their intelligence, soundness of limb and tough constitution, have always been favoured as foundation stock from which to breed larger ponies and horses. Nowadays there is a very high percentage of Welsh pony blood in children's riding and show ponies, particularly in the smaller ponies of under 13.2 hh (134 cms). There are still many herds living on the hills of Wales and many studs are now established outside Wales. Breeders still like to go back to Wales to buy stock from time to time to keep the type pure.

popular as ever. They are an ideal pony for trekking and trail-riding being strong, sure-footed and easy to handle. A Dales pony should not exceed 14.2 hh (144 cms) and should be black, dark brown, sometimes grey in colour but never chestnuts or odd colours such as skewbalds and piebalds.

To the south-west of England 1000 ft up on the rugged granite tors and windswept slopes live the Dartmoor ponies. A kind, intelligent breed of small riding pony that has lived on the wild moorland area of Dartmoor since the earliest times. In 1899, a Dartmoor section of the Polo Pony Society's (now the National Pony Society) Stud Book was established. The breed was defined by points, and that standard has remained virtually unaltered in the official description of the Dartmoor today.

They make perfect first ponies for children. Indeed they love children and seem to take a great interest in everything they do. They are kind and sensible and sturdy with excellent conformation and a good head-carriage that gives children confidence when riding them.

Not far away, on Exmoor, a wild expanse of moorland that stretches across the county of Somerset into Devon lives the Exmoor pony. Living side by side with red deer in one of the loveliest regions of western England, the Exmoor is one of the hardiest of the native breeds. Their toughness and honesty is recognized by breeders throughout the world especially in Canada and Denmark and their value as foundation stock is second to none.

Across the Bristol channel lies the Principality of Wales, home of the Welsh Mountain Pony and Cob. The Welsh pony is one of the most beautiful of the pony breeds, with its small, quality head, bold eye, and agile body. This breed has lived in the Welsh hills before history began. Its origins are lost in the mists of time but its reputation today for gentleness, courage and versatility is well known. The Welsh Mountain Pony should be between 12 hh to 13.2 hh (124 cms–134 cms) in height and the Welsh Cob anything from 13.2 hh–15 hh (134 cms–152 cms).

Writers of the time of King Canute (*c.* 995–1035) mention herds of wild horses living in a forest in the County of Hampshire in Southern England. These could have been the ancestors of the short-backed, hardy New Forest Pony. These ponies are now divided into two types (as many of the British Native breeds are); the first type ranges from 13.2 hh–14.2 hh (134 cms–144 cms) and the second type is up to 13.1 hh (133 cms). The ponies live as near to nature as any domesticated animal can, roaming the 60,000 acres of the New Forest, a heavily wooded area with open spaces covered with grass and heather.

Many of the British native breeds have benefited from time to time from the introduction of Eastern blood, particularly the New Forest Pony. In 1852,

Queen Victoria sent her Arab stallion, Zora to live in the forest for eight years. This is why the 'dished' Arab profile is a feature of many New Forest ponies.

Zora brings us to the exotic world of the Arab, one of the oldest clean-bred strain of horse in the world. The legendary Horse of the Desert has influenced practically every strain of riding horse throughout the world including the modern racehorse.

Such is the popularity of the Arab horse, and his perfection as a blood-line when crossed with other breeds, that he has indeed become a legend. Almost a fairy-tale, for in fact he does not originate from the Arabian peninsula. For, like the story of the 'true' horse and the creation of the Thoroughbred, the Arab's recorded history is full of contradictions and opposing theories.

Professor F. E. Zeuner in his book, *A History of Domesticated Animals* suggests that the equines of North Africa and the Middle East were Asses and Onagers only some 10,000 years ago whereas recog-

nizable horses or large ponies lived on the other side of the great mountain ranges that divided Europe from Asia and the Middle East. There is considerable evidence from archeological discoveries of Man's earliest settlements to back this up. Many historians, it seems, confused the Onager with the real horse. Professor P. K. Hitti, Professor Emeritus of Semitic Literature at Princeton University, in his *History of the Arabs* gives further weight to this theory saying, 'Renowned as it has become in Moslem literature, the horse was, nevertheless, a late importation into Ancient Arabia. This animal, for which the Najd was famous, was not known to the early Semites.'

While the first townsmen were struggling with the

Below: Arab mares and foals at the Emir's stud in Bahrein. The Arab, a horse of superb action, should trot like 'a deer trotting through fern'.
Right: The English Thoroughbred. To be eligible for entry in the General Stud Book an animal must be traceable to a strain already in earlier volumes, or have some 8 to 9 generations of pure blood.

Right: The Anglo-Arab is a horse of outstanding quality, successful as a hack, hunter, jumper and dressage horse.

Below: Four Don horses driven in a racing 'tachanka'. These famous Russian steppe horses are bred in the Don Valley. They are versatile horses, adaptable either to riding or driving, with characteristic heads. The Russian Army stud farms brought English Thoroughbred blood into the breed to create the Anglo-Don.

Far right: The Einsiedler is a breed of riding and draught horse, popular in the 16th century and a native breed of Switzerland. Many were stolen from the breeding stations after the French revolution and the English Hackney was introduced in the early 1900s to improve the breed. Now breeding is based on Anglo-Norman stallions.

sophistications of community politics and the slow process away from a 'hunting and gathering' economy, wandering Nomads were building up trade routes to the four corners of the Old World and perfecting the care and training of valuable herds of horses. Bands of horse-trading Celts, who sold horses to kings and princes as far afield as India and China, often settled in various states to work as mercenaries and horse-trainers. In many cases they would arrange for grooms and riders to stay behind and help their clients with horse-breeding and management.

The Nomadic tribes domesticated goats and sheep (and almost certainly the first pet or working dogs) but there is evidence that these decreased in size and shape with domestication whereas their herds of wild horses, nothing more than rough-haired ponies at first, actually increased and improved in size, shape and quality.

The civilized Urartians of the first and second millenia were natural horsemen. They were direct descendants of the warring-clans of nomadic barbarians and, it seems, the first of those groups to settle in one place. Urartu (now Turkey), their new homeland, was the land of horses. They were plentiful and the Assyrian Kings, travelled to Urartu to buy mounts for their massive cavalry units.

A king of the Mari (First Babylonian Dynasty) imported horses from as much as 200 miles (320 kms) away and the trade-routes with Asia Minor saw a very heavy traffic in horses. Then the Cassites, who sacked the great city of Babylon, left us the first written records of selective horse-breeding. For these people, the horse was not merely a noble and expensive beast but now a creature with his own pedigree.

So the weight of evidence shows that the Arab horse, or certainly his very close cousin, was brought to the Arab Peninsula by Man. The fascinating thing about the story of the Arab horse is that Man has continued to introduce the breed all over the globe with outstanding success. This attractive animal's versatility and adaptability are not only the secret to his immense popularity but also, the Arab's ability to be able to pass these qualities on to any breed or strain with which he is crossed.

There are many strains of Arabian horse today and stud books of the breed are kept in Argentina, Australia, Bulgaria, Canada, Egypt, France, Holland, Hungary, Japan, Pakistan, Poland, Rumania, South Africa, Spain, Turkey, the USA, the USSR and the United Kingdom. Among some of the oldest strains are the Polish Arab, a pure-bred strain first introduced to Poland in 1570. The Jordanian Arab, through over-selling and neglect, was at one time in danger of disappearing. The Royal Jordanian Stud, through hard-work, diligent research and enterprise, gradually built up a farm of superb horses with traditional narrow muzzles and high-set thick tails. They are all recorded 'asil' (pure-bred) and show the 'mitbah', characteristic arch at the top of the crest of the neck and the 'fiblah', the concave profile of the head which is more pronounced in mares. The Persian Arab is claimed by many experts to be the ancestor of the true Arabian horse. The Persians of nearly 3000 years ago enjoyed horse-racing so it is possible this ancient strain were the first racehorses used by Man. The Persian Arab stands a little taller than his other middle-eastern relatives, at around 15 hh (152 cms) but he has most of the Arabian qualities, large eyes, short alert ears, high tail-carriage, but he has a straight profile. The Royal Stud at Farahabad, just outside Tcheran, has a number of Persian Arabs, a strain well-known for their elegance, spirit and speed.

In modern Arabia, Kehailan is the principal strain, which to the Bedouin means 'nice eyes'. Bedouin buyers of Arabian horses look for a large pear-shaped eye with dark eyelids. This is one of the hallmarks of the pure Arab. Although there are no height restrictions, the average size is between 14.2 hh–15 hh (144 cms–152 cms) and the usual colours are varying shades of grey to pure white, chestnuts and bays.

The Arabian is one of the oldest established breeds in Australia, and the Arab Horse Society of Australia, based in New South Wales, is growing rapidly. Several thousand horses are now registered in the Australian stud book. The Australian Arab Horse Society is now the fourth largest in the world.

Nearly 11,000 pure-bred Arabians are registered each year in the United States with the International Arabian Horse Association and the Arabian Horse Registry of America. During the last decade Polish-bred horses and Egyptian blood lines have been

Far left: A Furioso-North Star stallion from the Furioso breeding farm, south of Budapest.
Left: The Golden Akhal-Teke, a saddle horse bred in Southern Turkmenia. It was one of the first of the Russian breeds of horse to get its own stud book. These 'desert-horses' whose purity of blood is carefully protected, have good bone and action. They are usually bay, grey or, as seen here, a golden shade with black or white points. They stand normally from 14.2 hh to 15 hh (144–152 cms) in height.

imported by breeders to stand at stud on the farms that flourish from Maine to California.

The classical conformation of the Arabian is a small fine head, deep chest, short back, high-set tail, clean, hard limbs and a 'floating' action. The face has a concave profile unlike his near-cousin the Barb. The 17th-century English breeder, the Duke of Newcastle said of this swift breed that came from the famous Barbary coast of Morocco, Algeria and Tunisia, 'Spanish horses were like princes, and barbs like gentlemen in their kind'.

The Barb, like the Arabian, is a desert horse, and originates from Morocco, Algeria and Tunisia. About 2000 years ago the region of the Moors was well-known for its horses. Scribes wrote of a 'dappled Moorish' breed of great stamina. When the Moslems over-ran Barbary some 700 years later they brought with them the desert-bred Arabian horse. These inter-bred with the native Barb and a small, light horse, standing about 15 hh, developed that had stamina and speed. The Barbary Coast was a very busy trading area in the 15th and 16th century and one of the most popular exports from the region was the flat-shouldered Barb with the 'ram-shaped head'. He travelled to Spain, Europe and Great Britain. They were sold in large numbers, so much so that they became very inferior as a breed and even up to the early years of the 19th century a Barb could be bought

anywhere in North-West Europe at a very low price. The true, pure-bred Barb is quite rare today, but the Government of Morocco and His Majesty King Hassan II's Royal Stud have done a great deal to re-establish the pure-bred Barb.

The Arab and the Barb were to play their part in the creation of the English Thoroughbred, the greatest racing machine on four legs.

It was in the early 17th century that James I took the first steps to creating the Thoroughbred for he purchased an Eastern stallion that had been imported from Constantinople with the idea of improving his Royal string of running-horses. The idea was not very successful but it did set a fashion that others were to follow with much better results.

In 1689 Captain Robert Byerley brought back to England an Eastern stallion that he had captured from the Turks at the Siege of Buda. This was the first of three Eastern stallions who are considered by most experts to have been the founding fathers of the modern Thoroughbred. Captain Robert rode his Byerley Turk at the Battle of the Boyne and this versatile horse went on to create the 'Herod' line, one of the most important in the breeding of the Thoroughbred racehorse.

The Byerley Turk's grandson, Tartar, a useful racehorse himself, sired Herod who was bred by the Duke of Cumberland in 1757. Herod became one of

the most successful stallions in thoroughbred history, begetting the winners of £200,000, an enormous sum in the 18th century. Many of the modern day classic winners of the racing world go back in a direct male line to Herod.

A few years later in 1704 a Yorkshire squire by the name of Richard Darley imported a stallion of the Managhi strain, one of the best breeds of the Anazeh Arabs. He became known as the Darley Arabian and he was responsible for two of the greatest Thoroughbreds of all time. His son, Flying Childers, raced by the Duke of Devonshire and described as, '. . . the fleetest horse that ever ran at Newmarket, or, as generally believed, was ever bred in the world,' and his great-great-grandson Eclipse, a brilliant racehorse who was never beaten on the turf. Over 100 of his descendants have won the English Epsom Derby.

Then in 1730 the Godolphin Arabian arrived in England via Paris surrounded by romantic stories. One story was that he had been found pulling a cart along the cobbled streets, another that he had been stolen. But, however, he was purchased by Edwin Coke, was generally accepted as a pure-bred Jilfan Arabian and later acquired by the Second Earl of Godolphin. The Godolphin Arabian established the important 'Matchem' line, an excellent honest horse whose progeny won £151,000.

But the story of the Thoroughbred is not quite so simple as that. Experts tend to be divided on the subject, some say the Thoroughbred's most important creative influence was the Eastern blood and some experts claim that the English origins are stronger. In fact, it seems to have been a bit of both. There is no doubt that the modern Thoroughbred, through his male line, traces directly back to these three great Arabian stallions. But clean-bred horses, particularly on the fertile pastures of the county of Yorkshire, were being produced before and during the importation of Eastern horses. Charles II imported or was given mares of Eastern blood that he added to his stock of home-bred mares that he had inherited. These became known as Royal mares and all Thoroughbred horses are descended, on their female side, from about thirty mares, some being Royal mares and others being pure native-bred mares. So the creation of the Thoroughbred might be more accurately described as a strong and influential injection of Arabian blood crossed with half-Eastern bred mares, home-bred native mares and, perhaps the most important of all, the climate and soil of England which, like Ireland, is well-suited to the raising of horses.

By around 1770 the English Thoroughbred had begun to establish himself and the importation of Arabians for the purposes of cross-breeding was gradually phased out for racing purposes.

In 1730 the first Eastern stallion arrived in the United States from England. His name was Bulle

Rocke and he was a son of the famous Darley Arabian. In those early days between 1665 and 1730 the American Thoroughbred was like his English counterpart – a cross between imported stallions or brood mares and local stock. Later in that century the English stallions, Medley, Diomed and Messenger arrived and created the legendary dynasties that now dominate the successful blood-lines of the American Thoroughbred. Sir Archie, foaled in 1805, and sired by Diomed was one of America's first great Thoroughbreds.

The breeding of Thoroughbreds in America is now an important industry but it is no longer confined to the traditional areas of Kentucky, Virginia and Pennsylvania as there are now major international establishments on the West Coast and in Florida operating with great success.

In 1799 the British Thoroughbred, Rockingham, was sent to stand at stud in New South Wales, Australia and so began the process that was to produce the Australian Thoroughbred. This breed is one of the toughest and most consistent racehorses in the world. In 1802, Northumberland, the first Thoroughbred stallion to be imported direct from England, arrived and an Arab called Nector arrived from Calcutta. Many Eastern stallions came to Australia via India. Along with Thoroughbreds they headed the lists of successful sires up to 1820.

Australia's near-neighbour New Zealand, with her perfect climate and soil conditions for the raising of clean-bred horses, produced three of the most famous and successful racehorses in the history of the Australian turf. They were the brilliant Thoroughbreds, Carbine, Phar Lap and Tulloch, that dominated the racetracks of Australasia between 1885 up to the 1950s. Carbine, a great track performer himself, sired the winners of over 200 races.

The Thoroughbred was not the only breed of horse to make the long journey to Australia for, as far as we know, the vast continent was never the home of a native wild horse. About 200 years ago the first European settlers created the state of New South Wales. They bred a horse by using Thoroughbred and Arabian stallions and he became known as the Waler after his State of origin. Nowadays the Waler is also known as the Australian Stock horse or the original cross-bred horse of the outback.

In America too, other breeds of horse came with the first settlers and have since developed into specialized breeds to suit the needs of the country. Here the Spanish influence was very strong. The horse had not been seen in the New World since the migration of the pre-history herds over to Asia and Europe. During the time of Christopher Columbus (c. 1446–1506) the Spaniards established horse-breeding centres in the West Indies. The taproot stock they used were Andalusian horses. In 1511

Top left: The Selle Français or French Saddle Horse, is similar to the successful Irish half-bred hunter. Since the Montreal Olympic Games of 1976, where the French team won the Team Show Jumping Gold Medal, and on his previous international competition record, the Selle Français has proved himself well.
Bottom left: The Hack is not a breed but a recognized and defined type of riding horse suitable for pleasure riding.
Top: The American Quarter Horse is at home roping, cutting or controlling cattle on the ranch. It was bred originally by early settlers in Virginia, USA by crossing a Thoroughbred stallion, Janus with native mares.
Above: The Pinto, or painted pony, was a great favourite with the North American Indian tribes because of his natural camouflage colouring.

Hernan Cortes, the first of the Conquistadores, took 16 horses to the American continent, the first to set foot there for thousands of years. They included 11 stallions, two Pintos and five mares. The Spaniards did everything possible to keep the horse out of the hands of the Mexican Indians but to no avail, for they soon obtained mounts. By the 17th century, nearly all the indian tribes of the Western Plains had horses. The Comanches and the northern Apaches were brilliant natural horsemen. Eventually European settlers also brought horses to the Atlantic Coast. Whereas in Europe, horses were used mainly for riding, in the New World of the Americas they were also used for light farm work, hauling and transportation. Often, one horse carried out several of these jobs as well as being used for riding.

The Paso Fino, an attractive small saddle horse originating from Columbia, Peru and Puerto Rico, is gaining in popularity. These are gaited-horses, like the American Saddlebred and the Tennessee Walking Horse, with specially defined paces, like the paso fino or fino-fino, a very slow gait with a great deal of collection and a steady unbroken cadence. The paso largo is another, a more relaxed gait, faster than a walk and with only light collection, suitable for trail or pleasure riding.

The Quarter Horse, the famous working horse of America, is a very popular breed in the USA. He is raced with great success over one quarter of a mile and can also be seen doing ranch work or competing at

**Top left:** The popularity of the handsome Tennessee Walking Horse now spreads far beyond his native Tennessee and North Carolina. This saddlehorse can now be seen from coast to coast in the USA.
**Below left:** A Morgan brood mare and foal, one of America's finest strains of riding horses. The Morgans originated in Vermont and New England and they all descend from the legendary 18th-century stallion, Justin Morgan.
**Right:** The Australian Pony was created through the importation of Welsh Mountain ponies which were bred with Arabians, Thoroughbreds, and Timor and Shetland strains. Australia has the largest Pony Club organization in the world.
**Below:** Waler mares and foals graze peacefully in New South Wales, Australia. Known as the Australian Stock Horse, its breeding and trueness to type is now controlled by the Australian Stock Horse Society.

shows in reining, roping and cutting classes. In 1973 there was a grand total of 931,112 Quarter horses registered in continental America against 612,759 Thoroughbreds, 199,200 Appaloosas, 391,970 Standardbreds, 107,000 Arabians and further down the list 51,291 Morgans and 21,583 Ponies of the Americas.

In Europe there are many breeds of horse that are indigenous to any one State or region. One of the most fascinating is the shortlegged and strong Noric horse. A breed of Bavarian and Austrian working horse that dates back to ancient times in the Roman province of Noricum. The Venetii, who lived just across the southern border of Noricum for some 900 years BC, were famous horse-breeders and produced the popular chestnut or palomino mountain pony known as the Haflinger. These hard-working ponies with flaxen manes and golden tails are branded with the national flower of Austria, an Edelweiss, with an 'H' in the centre.

In Hungary, Czechoslovakia, Poland and Rumania one of the most successful 'competition' horses is the handsome Furioso. In fact, he started out as an English half-bred in the old Austrian Empire and is still bred today in modern Austria. The original Furioso was imported from Britain around 1840 and from 1841 to 1851 he produced 95 stallions. Later the famous British stallion North Star, by a son of Touchstone out of a grand-daughter of Waxy, and thought to be of Norfolk Roadster blood, arrived in Hungary. Many of North Star's progeny found fame on the Hungarian trotting tracks. The Furioso-North Star is now generally accepted as one breed.

The Hucul of Poland, like the Konik (which means small horse), is one of the oldest strains of pony on the continent of Europe. He is a direct descendant of the original Tarpan which dates back to the Stone Age. For centuries they were used as pack animals carrying heavy burdens over rough mountain paths through snow, ice and thick fog. They now have their own central stud farm in Luczyna and are used as work-horses on the many highland farms of southern Poland.

In Germany the two most famous native breeds are the Hanoverian and the Holstein. Perhaps the most successful breed of light riding horse besides the Thoroughbred in the competitive worlds of dressage, three-day eventing and show jumping.

The Hanoverian, promoted by the ducal and later royal family of Hanover, was created by crossing native mares with Eastern, Spanish, Neopolitan and Thoroughbred stallions. The breeding of Hanoverians is now controlled by the Society of Hanoverian Warm-blood Breeders in Hanover and by the Westphalian Stud Book in Münster. One of the most

Left: A champion Dales pony. Dales are a native breed, originating in the eastern part of northern England. They are similar to, though slightly larger than, the Fell Pony of the western region of northern England. These strong ponies are workers, used for hundreds of years as pack animals. Some time ago, they were crossed with Clydesdales to increase their size but now they seldom measure above 14.1 hh (143 cms). The Dales pony is a sure-footed, active, versatile animal, suitable for riding or driving.

important stallion stations is at Celle with an affiliated stallion testing station at Westercelle, both situated in the region of Niedersachsen. The federal state of Northrhine-Westphalia serves the same purpose by providing young stallions in the stallion station at Warendorf which is also the home of the German National School of Equitation.

The origins of the Holstein, originally bred by Monks in the peaceful grounds of their monasteries, go back to the days of antiquity. Over the centuries Oriental, Neopolitan, Spanish, English and German Thoroughbred, and Yorkshire Coach Horse stallions have been used to improve and perfect the breed which is now successfully established as a very successful warm-blood multi-purpose horse that can gallop and jump exceptionally well. Meteor, the mount of Germany's Olympic rider and former European Champion Fritz Thiedemann was a Holsteiner.

The French Saddle Horse (Cheval de Selle Français) is the modern version of the Anglo-Norman and owes much of its present qualities to the Hanoverian, Holstein, Arab and English Thoroughbred blood that has been cross-bred into the breed. There are two types today, the Anglo-Norman draught horse in which Percheron and Boulonnais blood has been used and the, now very popular, Selle Français. The Anglo-Normans are mainly bred in the Mortagne region and the Selle Français in the Caen region where there are also many famous Thoroughbred and French Trotter studs.

The South of France is the home of one of the most ancient breeds, the Camargue horse. Now mainly a tourist attraction, these semi-wild horses that are left

Above: The Breton is among the best-known of the French heavy horses. They derived from both sides of the Black Mountains and spread over the Breton peninsula of Western France. They are well-made animals with a handsome head and a powerful, stocky body. They have great powers of endurance and plenty of liveliness. In North Africa, the Breton has been successfully crossed with native horses to produce a strain which is very suitable for the agricultural requirements of the region. Over the years, many foreign blood strains have been used to develop the breed, but the original character of the Breton has remained.
Right: The Noric horse is a small working horse used in Bavaria and Austria. There are two types, the Oberlander and the Pinzgauer. It is named after the kingdom of Noricum, part of the Roman Empire.

to breed naturally, were, and on occasions still are, stock-horses. The Gardiens, a type of French wrangler, used them for working with the black fighting bulls of the Camargue. It is thought that they are the fore-runner of the modern barb.

But perhaps the most international breed of riding horse in the world is the Anglo-Arab. There is hardly a country in the East, West, North or South that has not got a sizable population and a big following for these versatile riding horses.

The Arab Horse Society of England defines an Anglo-Arab as a cross from a Thoroughbred stallion and an Arab mare or vice versa, with their subsequent recrossing. In other words, they have no strains of blood other than Thoroughbred and Arabian in their pedigrees. In Australia, Canada and Sweden the same definition is followed. But in the USA not less than 25 per cent Arab blood nor more 75 per cent Thorough-bred is demanded. In France, South Africa and the USSR a minimum of 25 per cent Arab blood is required and in Poland $12\frac{1}{2}$ per cent Arabian.

Many Societies, especially the French, are now breeding larger Anglo-Arabs than in previous genera-tions. It is a strain of riding horse that provides the best of both worlds for the equestrian sportsman. He is full of quality with all that is best from the Thorough-bred but with the more classical head, stylish tail-carriage and intelligence of the Arab. In America,

Canada, Great Britain and Europe the Anglo-Arab is becoming increasingly more successful in the show ring and the demanding competition arenas of show jumping and three-day eventing.

In what was once the more practical area of the horse world, the heavy horse has become more of a show-piece than the important worker that he was in in the days of non-mechanized economies. From Britain the Shire, Suffolk Punch and Clydesdale, are now exported all over the world and are particularly popular in America. From France, the Percheron is also exported to the USA and has become well-established in Great Britain. The Percheron originated in the La Perche district of France about 100 years ago.

The Shire is by far the best loved and the best known of the heavy horses of England. A powerful, docile horse, the Shire stands over 17 hh (173 cms) in height and weighs around one ton to 22 cwts (1.016–1.117 tonnes) making him capable of hauling immense weights. The Shire was one of the finest working horses used in England before the Victorians adapted the economy to steam power, steel, and the combustion engine. It is thought that the amiable Shire, with his strong legs covered in fine silky hair, was a descendent of the Great Horse of Europe and was developed as a War horse. The theory being that as the medieval Knights must have weighed about 30 stone (420 lbs; 190.5 kg) in full armour they would have needed a horse of Shire proportions. But, however, it was found that the horse-armour that has survived through the ages could not have been made for a Shire horse or any other of his size as it is many times too small.

The medieval knights may have ridden a very, stocky, strong little horse but, although it may have

Below: The French Percheron is a rare mixture of power, beauty and grace.
Below right: A team of Clydesdales, a breed of heavy horse from the Clyde Valley, Lanarkshire, Scotland. This horse was originally bred from local mares and heavier Flemish stallions.

Right: A Shire enjoying a well-earned rest. Although this horse is grey, the colours are more usually bay and brown.
Below: The Suffolk Punch on show. These gentle, chestnut-coloured giants are famous for longevity and often work well into their twenties.

been a relation of his, it certainly was not the Shire or the Great Horse of Europe that thundered across the battlefields of days gone by, or galloped down the jousting lanes to win the favour of a Lady. It also seems that the much-loved cinematic scene of a Lord in armour being lifted onto his charger by some sort of crane was nothing more than artistic licence or fantasy.

Throughout the world people are now enjoying the pleasure that horses can give, not only by participating or spectating at sporting events but also through riding holidays, pony trekking, trail riding, Pony Clubs and Gypsy Caravan vacations. The immense variety of breeds and types that are now distributed throughout the world illustrate the fascinating results of evolutionary change. A long way to come, indeed, for a small creature that was no bigger than a dog.

# Horses at work

For thousands of years the horse has been a servant of Man. Great empires have been built or destroyed with the aid of the horse. Agriculture and commerce profited from his muscle and labour. Kings courted their queens with gifts of fine horses, envoys sealed inter-state treaties with the presentation of Royal stallions at court and mounted couriers carried, across vast distances, messages that would change the course of history. The horse brought Man from isolated communities into a wider world with lines of communication and trade routes. The horse provided Man with wealth, food, transport and power.

During the fascinating days of pre-history, the horse was the centre of many major cults. He was regarded as a beast of mystery and ritual rather than a beast of burden. The first settlers in the great valleys of the Nile and the Euphrates, fertile regions with ample vegetation, made the earliest known transition to an agricultural economy, harnessing the ox and the ass to plough their rich fields.

From what we know of the horse in those far off days there are several reasons why horses were not used for agriculture. Horses had to be imported in early times so were therefore expensive and were used only as mounts for the wealthy. The collar had not been invented, so that it was difficult to use horses for harness. Experts say that the collar was invented in China but it does not seem to have been used in Europe until Medieval times. Also, the wheel which revolved around its own hub on a greased axle had not yet been developed. Finally, we can add to that the fact that horses, at that time, were mere lightweight ponies. They were fleet of foot perhaps, but lacked the power to be worked in the fields or used for haulage.

It was the nomads of some 5000 years ago who first tamed, rode, bred and worked the horse. It was these same peoples that perfected the wheel by inventing spokes and the greased hub. The horse began to be used for light transportation. The chariot became the prized possession of the settled and non-settled peoples. It therefore follows that the horse's first role was in warfare. At first horses took chariots up to the battle lines and later became part of the massive cavalry units that were the war-machines of the early Assyrians and Barbarians through to the Huns, Celts, Visigoths, Moors, Crusaders and medieval kings.

**Left: An Aboriginal stockman and his cow-pony at work in the Australian outback. One can see the power in the pony's hindquarters as he 'takes-off'. The stock horse needs sharp acceleration, mobility and stopping power.**
**Right: Out on the prairie the horse and the herd are in their natural environment. Stock control and over-seeing was one of the first jobs which Man and horse carried out together. Here we can see the cattleman's Western saddle that allows him to ride with a straight, free leg in comfort over long distances.**

It was the civilized Romans and their civil engineers, however, that brought the horse into the more peaceful areas of Man's commercial activities. With their straight, hard-surfaced roads, horse-powered transport became an important part of the economy. They recognized the importance of horse transport and the need for a fast, efficient communications system. Roman couriers using teams of horses in relays harnessed to a light, four-wheeled cart would cover some 80 miles a day.

The agricultural horse came on to the scene working in the quiet, fields of medieval England. But, perhaps the oldest service, after warfare, which the horse has rendered to Man has been his use as a mount for the over-seeing and control of livestock. A partnership which the horse has contributed to for many thousands of years and one that has rightly earned a special place in the relationship between Man and Horse.

Some 160 years ago the light horses reared in New South Wales, then the only settled areas of Australia, became very popular as riding horses. They became

known as Walers after the name of the state where they were bred. Later, when Australia became a country of separate states, 'Waler' became the general term for the Australian-bred saddle horse. At first, Walers were a cross between Arabian, Thoroughbred and Anglo-Arab stallions with the best local mares. But with the passing of time the mares became more clean-bred until the early 1900s when the Waler was almost a clean-bred Anglo-Arab with strong Thoroughbred blood in him.

The Waler was, at one time, looked upon as probably the best saddle horse in the world. He served in cavalry units between Waterloo and the Crimean War. He served in India, Palestine and Syria during World War I. The Australian Desert Mounted Corps were mounted on Walers, but when hostilities ended, Australian quarantine regulations made it impossible for these horses to be shipped back home. Under orders from the government, most of them were destroyed in the desert. In Sydney a bronze memorial commemorates these horses that fought to free

Left: Driving a herd of cowponies towards the corral in Mesquite country. Many stock horses in America, Canada, Australia and Eastern Europe spend their early lives living in a semi-wild state.
Above: Stockmen urge a herd across a river during a cattle drive.

Palestine and defeat the Turks. The inscription reads: 'By Members of the Desert Mounted Corps and friends, to the gallant horses who carried them over Sinai desert into Palestine, 1915–1919. They suffered wounds, thirst, hunger, and weariness almost beyond endurance, but never failed. They did not come home. We will never forget them.'

By the mid-1930s, demand at home and abroad, for the Waler decreased and the breed in its pure form practically disappeared. But it re-emerged in the shape of the Australian Stock Horse, a Waler-type, that is the product of several crossings of blood, Thoroughbred, pony, Percheron, Arabian and Coach horse, giving a useful looking horse with stamina.

When the American Quarter Horse was first introduced, the Australian stockmen were furious that these importations should be thought to be superior to their station-bred stock horse. So, together with a group of enthusiasts on the eastern seaboard, they united to form the Australian Stock Horse Society. Their aim was to protect and encourage the breeding of the horse that, for generations, has been the backbone of the Australian cattle industry.

It could be said that the reputation of the American West was built on the back of a Quarter Horse. This compact, stocky cow-horse, so ideally suited in temperament and physique to working with the large beef herds of the western United States of America is, in fact, not a westerner. He is an easterner by birth, originating in the Atlantic seaboard settlements of the early British Colonists.

The North American pioneers found that they had unexpectedly inherited some quality 'native' horses left behind by earlier Spanish explorers. These they crossed with quality stallions imported from England and produced, with each subsequent generation, a superior type of versatile horse, well suited to the special demands of their 'frontier' life. These horses could tackle anything from jobs around the homestead, at the mill, haulage, take the family by carriage to the village church on Sundays and carry a man at a comfortable stride. Also they could be left to forage for themselves if necessary. Certainly, the Quarter Horse was the ultimate versatile mount.

The Quarter Horse has a highly sensitive instinct towards other animals and possesses an uncanny capacity for anticipating their actions. He can react almost instantly with a fast stop, a flash of acceleration, a mid-air turn, a swerve, a pivot on the hindlegs, with his body at seemingly impossible angles, in order to head-off or contain a wayward steer.

These brilliant horses are equally at home at work on the range, pleasure riding, trail riding, rodeo and western show competitions and, as we will see later, as a successful racehorse.

A near cousin of the Quarter Horse, by life-style if not by blood, is the Canadian Cutting Horse. These cow-horses, who have a reliable performance-record on the ranch, are also popular entertainers as competition horses. The Canadian Cutting Horse Association and the National Cutting Horse Association of Canada tells us that the contests are dramatic, thrilling and. . . . 'During the two and a half minutes . . . a rider demonstrates the ability of his horse to out-think the cow with terrific short bursts of speed, agility of turns in mid-air, fabulous foot-work, and co-ordination between horse and rider that is unexcelled in any arena event. . . . Once seen in action, spectators all over North America are amazed. . . . They all agree that to watch a Cutting Horse in action is indeed a spine-tingling experience.' The Quarter Horse and Cutting Horse contests in America are based, as are the Stock Horse classes in Australia, on actual ranch work.

In contrast to the rough and tumble of cattle-herding comes the elegant and rather superior American Saddle Horse and his close relative the Tennessee Walking Horse. These are horses of the plantations, practical, elegant, and in no shape or form resembling the horses of the rugged northern low-lands.

Just over a century ago, the region of the Ohio Valley gradually changed from a wilderness of forests and Indian settlements into an area of lush, rich plantations, almost feudal in social structure. The prosperous Southern Gentleman, a new aristocracy in a new world, looked for a horse that was both business-like and beautiful. A horse from which he could survey his crops, control his labour force and which would unmistakably identify his rank. The planters set out to create the ideal. They needed a horse that would be a comfortable ride during long hours in the saddle. Many of these wealthy men were in the saddle from dawn to dusk, and needed a horse with great endurance. Speed was of no special importance as the plantation bosses could not make efficient inspections at the canter. It took several generations of selective breeding, but the Kentucky horsemen managed to combine blood and quality to create an extraordinary horse, first known as the Kentucky Saddle Horse and now as the American Saddle Horse.

The Thoroughbred stallion Denmark, foaled in 1839, was the foundation sire of the breed but, apart from inherited flair and presence, there is nothing less like a Thoroughbred than the gaited-saddler. He is a tall horse, with a well-covered, rounded body, a high and naturally arched neck, a tail (which for show purposes is often artificially 'nicked') flagged high, strong,

sound-looking limbs with joints that move high, almost to a right-angle flexion. This action is rather similar to the English Hackney light harness horse and gives a slow, rocking action to his paces which are very comfortable for the rider.

The 3-Gaited Saddler performs at the walk, trot and canter and is shown with a roached (hogged) mane and the top of his tail close clipped with the rest 'pulled' thin. The 5-Gaited Saddler is the more dramatic of the three types. He is shown with full mane and tail and performs the simple walk, trot and graceful canter plus the slow-gait and the rack. The 'slow-gait' is a prancing action to a four-beat rhythm. As each hoof rises it remains momentarily suspended before striking the ground on one single beat. The 'rack' is the one that now thrills the show fans. It is a

**Right: An Australian farmer checks over his sheep at a muster. Some Australian farmers still prefer to use horses on their sheep and cattle stations. From the back of a horse he can examine his flock at a glance, picking out the lame or sick sheep. He is higher up than he would be sitting in a vehicle and, with his horse, he can also go into the flock without scattering them, or quickly round up the odd stray.**

very fast, fully extended version of the slow-gait. Five-gaited Saddlers have been known to cover a mile in 2.19 minutes at the rack.

The soft, flowing, non-bouncing Tennessee Walking Horse developed in Kentucky, Tennessee and Missouri in much the same way as the American Saddler. This time, however, the planters bred a horse that could half run, half walk—a real gliding horse, both gentle and relaxing. They were first known as Turn-Row horses because they were used for inspecting crops by rows.

These kind horses, one of the most amiable breeds, were not officially recognized as a breed until 1935. They may not be seen working on the 'rows' these days, but they are still very popular as they are ideal mounts for the nervous beginner wishing to take up horsemanship but who is a bit horse-shy. They are also useful for the competitive rider who wishes to leave the stresses and strains of the competition 'saddle' but still keep himself fit.

We cannot look at the horses of North America without including the fabulous Morgan, one of the most important strains of multi-purpose, light working horse. The Quarter Horse was the ideal in versatility but the adaptability and rags-to-riches history of the Morgan must make him one of the most fascinating horses in the world. He must be the only breed that is directly traceable to one unique 18th-century stallion.

In the early 1790s, a dark-bay two-year-old colt was given to Justin Morgan, an innkeeper in West Springfield, Massachusetts as payment for a debt. Justin returned with the colt to his home in Richmond

35

Centre, Vermont, and named him Figure. Morgan died of consumption shortly afterwards, however, and the colt changed hands many times, gradually slipping further down the ladder and performing even more menial jobs with each change of home. Eventually he was bought by Levi Bean, a farmer, and was allotted the lowly task of pulling the manure spreader.

During these hard times his name, Figure, was completely forgotten and he became known as 'Justin Morgan's Horse' and later quite simply as Justin Morgan. What is even more remarkable is that his breeding was also ignored. It is now thought that he was by a famous racehorse called True Briton. It has been established that at around the time of Justin Morgan's birth there was a stallion called True Briton. His dam is even more obscure but it is claimed she belonged, on her male line, to the same family sired by the imported stallion Wildair. This could be true, for Wildair was in the same ownership as True Briton. If this is so, Justin Morgan's dam is the direct maternal line from which the modern racehorses and stallions Nearco and Nasrullah were descended. There is also another story, however, which gives Justin Morgan's dam as just a humble mare from the Connecticut Valley.

In spite of all the conjecture we do know that this 'mighty atom' of a horse, who stood barely 15 hh and

weighed around 800 lbs had the constitution of an ox and the strength and spirit of a prize-fighter. He survived a lifetime of punishingly hard labour and poor treatment, working all the hours of daylight; pulling a plough, hauling loads through axle-deep mud, ripping roots and stumps from land being cleared for planting. When Justin Morgan was not working he was stood at stud for ridiculously low fees and was matched against all-comers in weight-pulling contests!

This remarkable horse also possessed a talent for speed. On high-days and holidays he was raced in harness and under saddle and was never beaten! His fame and that of his descendants spread all over New England. The Morgan of today may be taller and classier than little Justin but his heart and his spirit lives on in that fine brown frame.

Justin Morgan finished his days in service in the US Army, who established the Morgan Stud Farm. He died at the ripe old age of 32 years in 1821. During his long life he had established USA's most famous general-purpose horse that served in the cavalry, in the police service, the fire service, as stock horse and draught horse.

Great Britain and Europe are the homes of the more traditional heavy, working-horses like the Shire, Suffolk Punch, Clydesdale, Percheron, Irish Draught, Breton and the smaller dual-purpose working breeds like the Cleveland Bay, Hackney, Welsh Cob, native ponies, Haflinger and Fjord Mountain Pony. Many of the lighter, smaller breeds were working down coal mines or in tin mines until just before World War II but, thankfully, now most of them lead healthier lives as part of the new pastime of riding for pleasure that has grown so rapidly in the last 20 to 25 years. There was less mistreatment of ponies than was popularly supposed in their industrial days, indeed there are many examples of them having very special relationships with their handlers. Some of the pit ponies even retired with the men whom they worked with. But the horse, whether he be small, large, working or clean-bred, is a creature of the outdoors and it is preferable to see him in the countryside where he belongs.

Heavy breeds like the Shire, once the backbone of the European agricultural economy, are still as popular as ever, although nowadays they are mainly seen at country fairs or in the show ring. There are, however, still some farmers and commercial organizations who claim that the heavy horse is still economical on certain agricultural units and for short-haul transportation. They have one advantage in large towns over the motor-vehicle; you can't get a traffic fine for leaving

Above left: These Austrian Haflingers are performing the traditional task of pulling the hay-cart.
Below: The Fjord pony of Norway, like so many native breeds has some Arab blood in his veins. A feature is dun colouring and a black stripe down the back.

them at the kerbside! In many parts of continental and eastern Europe, the horse is still used for farming and haulage on hill-side or mountain-side holdings, or in forests, or on rugged terrain where wheeled vehicles can not travel.

In holiday centres on the south and north-eastern coasts of England, the Isle of Man or along the sun-scorched coast of the south of France, the carriage horse still plys for trade along the promenades or in the parks.

The Hansom cab, forerunner of the taxi cab of our cities, was a two-wheeled vehicle with the driver seated high up at the back. It was originally designed by an architect named J.A. Hansom in 1834 as a large, clumsy carriage. It was later modified into the popular shape by Mr. J. Chapman. The Hansom cab, a regular sight in 19th century London, was a public cab for hire and known as 'the gondola of London'.

The Hackney horse is an immediate descendant of the world-renowned Norfolk Trotter. This horse, later known as the Norfolk Roadster, was powerful, well-built, bred by England's shrewd East Anglia farmers for use in their daily work. They had great stamina and powers of endurance. They often took the farmer and his family to market but, with the coming of the steam railway in the 19th century, the Roadster fell out of favour. The breed was revived later by the Hackney Breed Society. The Hackney Pony, a smaller version of the Hackney Horse, was used up to the

beginning of the 20th century, by many tradesmen for making deliveries. These attractive, proud horses and ponies have a natural gait at the trot that has a spectacular action. The shoulder movement is free with a high, ground-covering knee action and a slight suspension that gives the action grace. The action must be true and straight with no dishing or throwing of the hooves from side to side.

One of the last working horses before the age of mechanization, to whom we owe a great debt, was the Fire Horse. The first fire horses were used by Augustus in 21 BC when he assembled a team of 600 men as fire fighters. The appliances used in ancient Rome were not very different from the equipment we use today. They had pumps, leather fire buckets, picks for pulling down burning buildings, woollen cloths soaked in vinegar as fire extinguishers, ladders, jumping sheets. These were all rushed to the scene of the fire on horse-drawn currus, or tenders, while the firemen ran behind it as fast as they could. They must have been fitter than the horses!

The first steam fire engine was made by Messrs Braithwaite and Ericson of London in 1829 and it was horse-drawn. The manual engine however continued to be widely used through the 1860s and 1870s in Great Britain and America. As the fire bell rang out its urgent call, the fire horses would race like chargers into battle, sparks rising from their iron-clad hooves as they clattered over the cobbled streets, with their heads tossed high and their manes flowing.

They were cavalry-type horses, specially trained for fire fighting. The London Metropolitan Fire Brigade was established in 1886 and all the fire engines and escapes were horse-drawn. The ideal age for a fire horse was said to be from 4 to 7 years. The officer's trap horses were well-bred pacers capable of trotting a mile in 3 minutes. In the country areas, local horses were taken from bridal carriages or hearses to 'volunteer' for the fire wagon in cases of emergency.

Although it has moved now into history, the fire horse served with valour and to the highest principles of the long tradition of the working horse—Man's longest serving and most generous working partner.

**Below:** Heavy horses still work in the great forests of Canada and Australia, hauling timber down to the mills.
**Right:** Two heavy horses, Major and Violet, pull the plough across an English field as their ancestors have done for centuries. These large, attractive and docile animals are still very popular.

# The horse at rest and play

The horse is an animal of the outdoors. The wide open spaces are the natural kingdom of the horse. The herd, with its daily code, social structure and discipline, is his community. This creature of immense strength, and ability, many times more powerful and quicker than Man is one of nature's pacifists. Never in his long and fascinating history has the horse been the aggressor. Within his own herd he may attack younger members to discipline them, or occasionally, two stallions may fight over the possession of mares.

The horse has always been a vegetarian. He has never eaten the flesh of any other member of the animal kingdom. Horses do not have any special means of attack or defence such as sharp teeth, claws, horns or antlers. They rely on alert ears, quick eyes, a good memory and the speed to out-run most of their natural enemies.

Before being domesticated, the wild horse lived a simple life. The herd was led by a stallion who was, within the group, the dominant and most positive member. He led his herd of mares and young over the grasslands in search of good pastures. The stallion was ever alert, watchful for danger from predators or rival stallions. The strongest and most intelligent stallions won the largest and best herds of mares so that their ability was passed on through their offspring.

The young foal started life as a timid, fragile creature feeding from his mother and following wherever she or the rest of the herd went. Gradually his body became stronger and soon he was feeding himself and beginning to identify and relate to the other youngsters in the herd. These youngsters, colts and fillies, played and grazed together. Sometimes they would chase each other and stage 'mock' fights rearing up and striking at the air in front of them. Often, they would just run, in a group for sheer 'joie de vivre'. As the seasons passed, the youngsters would gradually begin to take life more seriously. The constant movement through forests and over mountain ranges would involve walking, trotting, making quick changes of direction and galloping to safety. All the time, life within the herd, both playful and serious, was preparing the young horse for maturity. His body and mind soon developed to cope with his new responsibilities and the demands of his life within the herd. Natural selection removed the weak and the ailing,

**Top left: Young Thoroughbreds on the Ocala Stud in Florida. They chase each other around and try to out-run each other. These yearlings are not only having fun but they are also preparing their bodies for a career on the race track.**
**Left: A superb Palomino stallion, the 'Golden Horse of the West' provides a beautiful picture that epitomises the spirit of the horse at liberty— proud, muscular and confident.**
**Right: Horses love to roll in the paddock particularly after a day's work.**

Above: A herd of wild white Camargue horses enjoy a gallop across the shallows of the Rhône in southern France.

leaving only the strongest and fittest who could survive the daily hazards.

Almost throughout the entire world, Man has domesticated this powerful and beautiful creature. The horse has adapted himself to this new situation by substituting co-habitation with human-beings for the life of the herd. He looks to Man as he did to the stallion as protector and provider. Many horses have been known to show tremendous loyalty and affection to one man or to a family.

In removing the horse from his natural environment, Man has created problems for him that would not normally have entered his life. This particularly applies to horses which are kept in stables. Brood mares and the sturdy native horses and ponies are usually well adjusted as they frequently live out in the open fields where they can exercise and amuse themselves.

One of the biggest problems for the stabled horse is boredom and loneliness. Horses love company. Even domesticated horses still possess a strong herd instinct. Yet we often put them into a loose-box where they can only see one or two other horses, or, what is worse, nothing to look at but a blank wall. This is how so many of the terrible stable-vices come about—from loneliness and boredom. Too often one sees fit, trained horses, both young and old, left in their loose-boxes on their own for most of the day. When this occurs, horses frequently develop odd habits and tricks to amuse themselves.

Rug-chewing is a common stable vice. Young horses will do this, especially at night. They will either chew at the front of their rug or try to pull it off completely. This is caused purely and simply by boredom. The answer? Get the horse out as much as possible, work him more, get him more occupied, and, if possible, leave his rugs off for a while until he is more settled when left alone. Muzzles can be used to stop this sort of thing but the trouble with muzzles and other restrictive pieces of equipment is that they will often turn a horse sour and lead to far more serious vices.

The two greatest evils to affect the stabled horse are crib-biting and weaving. Both are caused through

boredom and loneliness and, sadly, they can be hereditary. Crib-biting is perhaps the worse of the two. The horse puts his teeth over the manger or the bottom half of his stable door or any other protruding ledge and literally bites on it. At the same time taking air into his lungs and grunting. It soon becomes a nervous habit, rather like nail-biting, which is almost impossible to break. There are certain pieces of equipment, like a crib-biting device, or nasty-tasting substance that can be painted on the doors etc. But most of them do not actually cure the vice in the real sense. Weaving is also a nervous problem. The horse rocks to and fro continually and will eventually start lifting one forefoot, then the other, to the rhythm of his weaving. Obviously it affects the horse's well-being and, like crib-biting, it will be difficult to keep the horse in good condition.

Another bad habit which can follow on from crib-biting is wind-sucking. The horse stands in his box sucking in air and swallowing it with a gulping sound. The horse eventually loses his appetite and his condition deteriorates. The great problem with these

vices is that is it often inherited and also young horses stabled near an affected horse will tend to copy it. Before long the entire stable yard is crib-biting or wind-sucking. It is a sorry sight to see and purely and simply caused through absolute boredom and nothing else. It is the fault of the horse's owner or trainer if an animal develops these vices which, once present, are almost impossible to cure.

Azoturia, or as it is often termed today, Haemoglobinuria, is a sickness that can affect the stabled horse. It occurs when well-fed horses are kept in their boxes too long with insufficient exercise. The horse suffers pain, sweats a lot, and is acutely lame. The horse lies down in his box seeking some form of comfort but once down he is unable to get up again. Azoturia can be fatal but if the horse is got up and gently encouraged to move out into the stable yard, the condition can be cured. Often, however, horses that do recover are left with a permanent damage to their muscles. This condition would not arise if the horse is given plenty of exercise and kept in a field as much as possible.

Let us, however, turn to a brighter topic—the horse at play. And he *is* playful, with a great sense of fun. Racehorses are possibly the most humorous of all domesticated horses. They live in a world that is nearer to their own natural lives. The racehorse uses his most natural talent—speed. In return for his labours he is looked after like any other athlete. In the majority of stables the routine is geared to his welfare and his enjoyment. For he is the asset of the yard. The stable staff tend to build a special relationship with the horses that are trusted to their care.

There are many stories in racing of famous horses that have travelled from one country to another. An occurrence which is not uncommon in today's 'jet-age' world of international racing. A top track performer can often, after his career as a three-year-old ends, find himself suddenly being shipped from France to America, to stand at stud or to continue his racing career as a four-year-old or five-year-old. Often it is found that he literally pines for the company of his regular handler and will continue to be upset until that man or girl is also shipped out to join him.

Brown Jack, one of the greatest stayers in the history of British racing, was a great character. He and his jockey, the legendary Steve Donoghue, had an almost uncanny understanding. This situation captured the imagination of their vast public following. Steve Donoghue often said that Brown Jack was intensely curious. If he was not ridden strongly enough even if he was in front, he would often slow down to a canter and gaze into the stands. Brown Jack also had a

Left: A herd of Lipizzaners enjoying the freedom of their semi-wild lives. Many of the darker-coloured youngsters will turn to the traditional grey colour at maturity.

peculiar shuffle which he made just as he came to the winning post. Donoghue said that Brown Jack hated straight courses because they were not sufficiently interesting for him and enjoyed the course at Ascot very much. Brown Jack and Steve Donoghue won the Queen Alexandra Stakes at Ascot six years in succession (1929–1934).

The 1934 classic horse Windsor Lad, and the great steeplechaser Arkle, winner of nearly £80,000 in stake money, were excellent examples of just how extrovert the Thoroughbred can be. Windsor Lad used to stop while cantering to the starting post. He would cock his ears and stand and have a good look at the crowd. Then off he would canter again towards the starting post. Arkle, too, used to do this but his sense of humour really came out on important occasions. He was so popular with the race-crowds that they would cheer him as he came up to the stands on his first circuit. Arkle would wait until he arrived at a fence which was directly in front of the crowd and would suddenly make a huge, exaggerated leap over the fence. The crowd would applaud wildly and Arkle seemed to understand and enjoy it.

The most enjoyable time in a racing stable is when the 2-year-olds and yearlings begin their early training. In Great Britain this is normally in the autumn. The mornings are beginning to become a little more crisp and the wind blows a little harder at this time of year. The youngsters are in high-spirits each morning and as they follow each other crocodile style up to the gallops it only takes the sight of a partridge popping up out of the long heathland grass, for one of the colts to whip round. In a moment the excitement runs right down the string and tails flash and heels glint as the lively youngsters bounce and plunge in all directions, uttering excited squeals and tipping their riders on to the dew-covered turf. The young Thoroughbreds seem to have a definite twinkle of amusement in their brown eyes as they survey the scene of crumpled, cursing stable lads picking themselves up from the ground. Horses are great mimics and there is nothing a young racehorse enjoys more than taking a cue from

the horse in front of him often adding his own little tricks to the game. If the other horse whips round to the left he will decide to go to the right. If one decides to put in a little jump and kick before going onto the training track another will jump into the air and outdo his fellow with two, good, hearty kicks. This is part of the fun and fascination of working with young Thoroughbreds. You never quite know what is going to happen next.

A lively wind, is to the young horse, what a rubber ball is to the human youngster—something to be kicked around a bit. Whether he is in the paddock or out on exercise there is nothing he enjoys more than turning his back-end into the wind and taking playful kicks at it. Some young horses, particularly colts, will stand up on their hindlegs and paw at the wind. It all helps to keep their minds occupied and it certainly keeps the stable lads awake.

As well as becoming attached to the people they work with, racehorses also get very attached to various other animals that can be found around a stable yard such as cats, dogs, chickens and birds. There are many stories in the racing world of crack performers who would not load up in the motor horse box to go to the races without their companion which may be a goat or a donkey. There was one famous hurdle racer in England that would not go anywhere, even on a trip to France, without his close companion, who was a goat. The trainer had to enlarge his loose-box at home to accommodate both of them and then arrange for the same thing to be done at any racecourse where the horse was running. Without the goat the horse literally became a nervous wreck!

**Above:** A fine-looking brood mare and foal enjoy a good canter across their paddock.
**Right:** Horses and ponies love company and, in general, will live amicably with other horses or with sheep, goats or cattle.

# The horse on show

The horse has not only played a part in warfare, agriculture and industry but has also contributed to the colour and pageantry of our daily lives. Nothing, as yet, has replaced the horse in the part he plays in traditional ceremonies and traditional festivals.

At the Spanish Riding School in Vienna the horse, the Lipizzaner, still has the leading role. The school, which dates back originally to the 16th century, is the home of classical riding and training. Here, equitation is practised and taught on the same lines as it was by the great Italian and French Riding Masters of the 16th and 17th centuries. While the School is on its annual tour abroad, equitation can be seen throughout the world in its purest form. All the classical High

School and Dressage movements are displayed in their repertoire, including the Levade. Here, the horse raises his forefeet off the ground, folds them up, while his hindquarters deeply bent support the entire weight of his body. In the Capriole, the horse makes a half-rear with his hocks drawn well under him and flexed, then he explodes into the air with a forward jump of some considerable height. While in the air, he kicks out energetically with his hindfeet before landing balanced and collected on four legs. Another movement is the Courbette, where the horse takes the attitude of almost the full rear, jumps forward off his hocks and lands again with the hocks still flexed and, still in the rearing attitude, takes several bounds.

**Left: Riders of the Spanish Riding School enter their baroque arena mounted on their famous 'white' Lipizzaner stallions. The Riders, in their 18th-century bi-corn hats, brown frock coats and high riding boots, give public displays of classical equitation based on principles that have existed for over 400 years.**
**Right: The streets of Seville, Spain, become a scene of colour and splendour during the famous Seville April Fair. Besides being a horse-market, it is also a gay fiesta with horsemen riding Carthusian and Arab horses through the decorated streets accompanied by attractive girls.**

The school gets its name 'Spanish' from the Anda-lusian, Arab and Barb horses that were imported from the Spanish Court of Queen Isabelle in the 16th century and from which the Lipizzaner horse derives. The school is situated in the Imperial Palace, once the home of the Emperor Charles VI, right in the city centre of Vienna. The baroque, galleried riding hall lit by chandeliers, is some 180 ft (54.8 metres) long. On the archway over the two entrance doors is the inscription, 'This imperial Riding School was built in the year 1735 upon order of Emperor Karl the 6th, son of the late Emperor Leopold I, for the education and training of noble youths and for the training of the horses for equitation and war. . . .'

The first director of the school was Max Von Weyrother. Today's director is Col. Karl Albrecht. The staff of the school nowadays are civil servants, who work to achieve the rank of Rider which can take some ten years to attain. Chief Rider is Ignaz Lauscha. He has five Assistant Riders who work with him training the horses, producing the displays (there are two public performances per week at the school for eight months of the year) and to train the occasional pupils taken at the school. The Riders wear long boots, brown frock coats and 18th-century bi-corne hats.

Originally during the Hapsburg Empire, the Lipizzaner horses used by the school were bred at Lipizza. Since 1920, however, they have been bred at the Piber Stud in Western Styria, near Koflach. The breed was founded by the Archduke Charles, son of Emperor Ferdinand I of Austria, around the year 1580. It was he that imported Spanish, Italian and Arabian horses to create a high-quality parade horse. The breed takes its name from Lipizza. Lipizzaners are blessed with a quiet, amiable character, long, well-developed bodies with short crested necks and short legs. From the Spanish horse they have inherited large intelligent eyes set in a convex face. Lipizzaners can be of any colour but the Spanish Riding School only uses grey stallions.

The future of the Riding School was severely endangered during World War II. If it has not been for Col. Alois Podhajsky and the US army commander General Patton, we may never have been able to see

**Left: A Hackney harness horse shows his paces at the famous Show held by the Royal Agricultural Society of New South Wales in Sydney.**
**Below: Australian children at a Pony Club rally. Australia has one of the largest Pony Clubs in the world.**

the famous 'Ballet of the White Horses'. During World War II the horses were moved out of bomb-torn Vienna to Upper Austria. In the turmoil of 1944 Col. Podhajsky placed his precious Lipizzaners under the protection of the United States Army. During 1945 General Patton returned them to Vienna to continue their tradition of some 400 years of classical equitation.

The Spanish Riding School is not the only centre that continues the traditions of the Renaissance Riding Masters, for the Cadre Noir of France is also internationally known for its fascinating displays of Haute Ecole and advanced riding and training. The Cadre Noir are a group of riding instructors from the celebrated French cavalry school of Saumur. In their smart black uniforms, they were once part of the Cavalry School. These talented horsemen are attached to the Institut National d'Equitation (a half civilian, half military organization) which is now the Ecole Nationale d'Equitation. Its purpose, besides producing the Cadre Noir displays, is to train civilian instructors and coach advanced competition riders.

Not far away from the quadrilles and displays of the Spanish Riding School and the Cadre Noir are the dramatic and exciting spectacles of the Gun Carriages

of the British King's Troop, Royal Horse Artillery, and the Musical Rides of the Household Cavalry and the Royal Canadian Mounted Police. The King's Troop, who provide the horse-drawn guns that are fired on the Queen's birthday, are based at St John's Wood and can often be seen exercising in Hyde Park, London. The Household Cavalry provide Queen Elizabeth II's mounted escort on ceremonial occasions such as the drive on the day when Parliament is opened and the mounted guard which can be seen at the entrance to Whitehall, London.

The Royal Canadian Mounted Police, the celebrated 'Mounties', provide one of the most fascinating Musical Drives in the world. Large audiences turn out to watch them at military tattoos, horse and agricultural shows and state fairs. Perhaps their most famous venue is the 'Calgary Stampede' staged in Alberta, Canada. Riding their Canadian-bred Thoroughbreds, they wheel and weave into formations, until eventually they form the Maple Leaf, Canada's national emblem. Their finale is a hair-raising lance-charge across the arena.

The Calgary Stampede is perhaps one of the world's most exciting equestrian spectacles. It is held each year in July and is Canada's top rodeo. Crowds flock to this unique show and thrill to the drums,

dancing Indians, the Thoroughbred racing and, most popular of all, the Chuck Wagon races. These are based in the pioneer days when settlers, under sudden attack from Indians, would throw all their equipment, including the cooking stove, into the back of the wagon, then with four horses pulling the covered vehicle, race for safety. The Calgary Stampede also includes bronc riding, bare-back bronc riding, steer wrestling, calf-roping, wild horse racing, wild cow milking, Brahma bull riding and even wild buffalo riding!

In Spain, Portugal and Southern France the bull-fights and the wine festivals attract the crowds and the horse is once more in the spotlight. The horses are often Andalusians, one of the most popular breeds of riding horse in Spain. They were originally known as Iberian (Spanish) but after successful cross-breeding with the Barb they took their present name from the province, in the south of Spain, where they were bred.

In the 14th century, performing horses were popular in the travelling circuses of Medieval England. There are three types of circus horse and, basically, three types of equestrian acts. Liberty horses perform movements and 'tricks' unridden. They usually perform in groups of 6 to 16 or more. There is also the Haute Ecole horse, which is often ridden solo or in

Left: These immaculately turned-out Life Guards with their handsome, well-matched mounts are a popular attraction at Horse Guards Parade in London.
Right: The Musical Rides of the Royal Canadian Mounted Police are legendary. Precise training and faultless turn-out make this team of horsemen famous throughout the world. Here a 'Mountie' finishes preparing his equipment ready for parade.

twos or threes. They perform the Pas de Deux or Trois, a programme of advanced movements based on the age-old traditions of the classical High School. Lastly there are the Rosinbacks, the stocky, strong, beautifully balanced horses used by the bare-back riders. They get their name from the resin that is rubbed on their backs to prevent the performers from slipping. The bareback riders are trained by using a Rosinback Riding Machine. This is a crane-like apparatus that supports a rope which is fixed to a leather belt around the performers waist. This prevents the rider from having a heavy fall if he loses his balance.

Finally we look at the Show Ring, the elegant arena that shows off native breeds, show horses and hunters, heavy horses, driving horses, donkeys, ponies, young stock and show jumpers from every nation. In America, the American Horse Shows Association is the controlling body of all recognized shows in the United States and, like the British Horse Society and British Show Jumping Association and other National Federations, it produces a register of judges and pub-

**Above: The London Harness Horse Parade Society, founded in 1966 but with associations going back to 1890, organizes the annual Harness Horse Parade every Easter Monday in London's Regent's Park.**
**Right: Bavarian Brewery horses dressed up in their highly decorated harness for the Munich Oktoberfest.**

lishes annually a Rule Book.

The US National Horse Show is staged each year in November at Madison Square Garden, New York City. The 'Garden' or 'The National' as it is often called was founded in 1883 and is America's premier show. At the Garden, the classes include divisions for harness, equitation and international show jumping.

Throughout America and Canada, the state fairs, agricultural shows and horse shows provide a vast panorama of horses of all shapes, sizes and disciplines. One can see the brilliant Saddlehorses, Walking horses, Stock horses, 'green' and 'open' hunters, ponies, carriages and show jumpers. The 4-H Clubs (Head, Hands, Heart and Health) are for farmer's children but their activities cover more than just equitation. Cattle, sheep, hogs, poultry, field crops

and handicrafts all form part of the programme. They stage horse shows in every state with divisions for English Saddle riding and Western Saddle riding.

In Australia, the Royal Sydney and Royal Melbourne are the major shows and here, classes for the Australian Stock horse are just as popular as the traditional show classes and the very competitive show jumping. The Equestrian Federation of Australia has its headquarters at the Royal Show Ground, Ascot Vale.

In Ireland, the Royal Dublin Show is mecca to all horsemen and enthusiasts, while in England the county shows form the basis of the 'circuit'. The Royal Show is held at Stoneleigh in the Midlands, the Royal International Show and the Horse of the Year Show are held in London each year. Together with the All England Jumping Course at Hickstead in the south, all these shows are the highlights of the British horsemen's year.

# Equestrian sports

## Polo

We do not really know where and when polo began as a game but the earliest records show that the game existed in some form in 525 BC. The birthplace of polo seems to have been ancient Persia, where a game similar to lawn tennis, called Chaugan, was played mounted. The origins of the modern game came from India, a popular pastime of the rich Maharajas and British Army officers. It was the 10th Hussars who brought the game to England and the first game was played in public at Hounslow, just outside London in 1869. The game was already being played by Assam tea planters in 1850 and it was introduced into North America in 1883.

The oldest Polo Club is the Indian Cachar Polo Club, which was founded in 1859 by a group of British planters in Assam. This fast, exciting game is now played in many countries and their clubs are affiliated to the Hurlingham Polo Association. Although polo is no longer played at Hurlingham the London committee still holds jurisdiction over many clubs outside England.

In the United States, the game did show signs of losing popularity but under the control of the US Polo Association popularity is again increasing. In 1972 there were 129 member clubs, including outdoor and indoor clubs. The two major matches in America are the National Handicap of 20 to 25 goals and the National Open for 18 to 22 goals. Both matches are played at Oak Brook, Illinois. Other important matches are played in some 20 or more states of the Union.

Australia, too, has its important clubs and matches under the Australian Polo Council. In Britain, now accepted as the home of the game, huge crowds flock to see the players at the Cowdrey Park Polo Club, the Guards Polo Club, Cirencester Park Polo Club, the Rutland Polo Club and others dotted around the country.

The polo field is laid out on a flat piece of ground which usually belongs to a club. It measures 300 yds (274 m) in length by 160 yds (146 m) wide if boarded or 200 yds (182 m) wide if unboarded. The polo boards must not exceed 11 ins (27.9 cms) in height and

**Left:** Two polo-players battle for possession of the ball. A popular sport, polo is now played throughout the world.
**Right:** The run for the wire at Aqueduct, New York State. The modern jockey's crouching seat and short stirrup leathers were originated by the American jockey James Todhunter (Tod) Sloan (1874–1933). He introduced his forward seat to Britain in 1897. Tod's 'invention' revolutionized race-riding techniques and is now used universally for flat- and hurdle-racing.
**Overleaf:** Pairs show-jumping classes are quite popular in hunter trials. Being sociable animals, ponies enjoy jumping together and encourage each other.

Left: The grace, freedom and style of the American team riders is an exciting spectacle. Here, Mary Chapot and White Lightning are seen jumping at Hickstead.
Above: Brazilian rider Nelson Pessoa, now based in France, is one of the most stylish riders in the world. Pessoa has won the British Jumping Derby twice and Germany's Hamburg Derby four times, all on the grey Gran Geste.

are fixed on either side of British and American grounds. There is a safety zone of 10 yds depth running down both sides of the playing area and of 30 yds depth behind each of the goal areas. In the USA and Argentina, the ground dimensions are sometimes larger. The goal posts are 8 yds (7 m) apart.

Each player is handicapped (on an 8-chukka basis) from minus 2 up to 10 goals (the best players). The aggregate handicap of the four players in a team is the team handicap. In all matches played under handicap conditions during the season, the higher handicapped team shall concede to the lower handicapped team the difference in the handicaps. This is divided by six and multiplied by the number of periods of play of the match.

In Argentina, a full game is 8 chukkas, but only 6 in Great Britain and the USA. Each chukka is timed to last 7 minutes. A bell is then rung but play continues until the ball has gone out of play or until the umpire decides it is fair to both sides to stop play. In the event of a draw, the game continues with extra chukkas until the winning goal is scored. There is a 3 minute interval between chukkas and 5 minutes at half time. After each goal is scored, the both teams of 4 players change ends.

The polo ponies normally play 2 chukkas in one afternoon with a rest of at least one chukka in between. There is no height restriction on the ponies and the term 'pony' is still used even though some of them are small horses. Today, most of the ponies come from Argentina, one of the sport's leading nations. Many have more than a sprinkling of Thoroughbred blood in their veins. They have to be extremely quick, agile and courageous.

The players wear brown top boots, breeches, and usually a light sweat-shirt. They also wear pads for protection, for polo can be rough and dangerous. The ponies wear protective boots and bandages on all four legs. For safety the players also wear a polo cap, a form of crash helmet. The polo stick, or mallet, is about 51 ins (129 cms) long, but there is no hard and fast definition as to its shape and size. The polo ball is around $3\frac{1}{4}$ ins (8.25 cms) in diameter and weighs between $4\frac{1}{4}$ to 5 ozs (127–141 g). The ball is made of willow and bamboo, but the practice ball is made of unburstable foam rubber.

Polocrosse is very popular in Australia. It is a mounted combination of polo and lacrosse. It began as an indoor game in England in the 1930s. In Australia, where the game was first played in 1939, there are three players in a team riding ponies restricted to 15 hh (1.52 m) in height and using a polo-type stick with a net on the end and a soft ball. The playing field is 160 yds (146 m) by 60 yds (54 m), and the goal posts are 14 ft (4.27 m) high and 8 ft (2.43 m) apart.

### Flat-racing

The sport of horse-racing caused the development of one of the finest and purest strains of horse found in the world today, the Thoroughbred. Man has raced horses since the Greeks introduced the sport to the Olympic Games over 2600 years ago. Racing was very popular in Roman-occupied Britain. Later, in the early part of the 16th century, there was organized racing staged at York, in the north, and Chester, in the west. It is recorded that Queen Elizabeth I went racing at Salisbury during the year that her navy conquered the Spanish Armada.

Organized popular racing began with the Stuarts, for it was James I who first created Newmarket, in eastern England, the sporting centre for horse-racing. James I also started the fashion of using Eastern blood to improve the native running horses. James I was, however, more of a hunting enthusiast so that the matching of racehorses was still, as yet, a private sporting affair rather than a public one.

Charles II, a true, sporting gentleman, loved racing, gambling and women. He bred, owned, and sometimes rode some of the best horses of the day. He created the Round Course and some form of organized system at Newmarket, now the headquarters of British Racing. In 1665 Charles II created the Newmarket Town Plate, a race which he himself won twice. No trainer, jockey, stable lad or groom can ride in this race which is run over 4 miles (6.4 km) on the Round Course. Amateur lady-riders are eligible to ride in the race which, at one time, was the only race in England open to ladies. The race is still run, but it has become a little gimmicky with all sorts of unusual prizes such as pounds of sausages!

Racing in those days was simply a question of matching two or three horses against each other for a sizable purse or side-bet, or both. The matches were run in punishing heats usually over 4 miles (6.4 km). There were occasional professional trainers and riders,

but it was mainly a 'gentleman's' sport, although gambling and cheating were furious! Eventually, a group of men, with rank, wealth and enthusiasm, got together to form the Jockey Club. This is a sort of committee dedicated to bring a set of rules to the game and to keep a respectable image. Over 200 years later, the Jockey Club is still the governing body of racing in Great Britain.

In 1752, the Jockey Club first established itself with a plot of leased land at Newmarket which later was to house the present Club rooms. A Mr Weatherby started the General Stud Book in 1791 and a relation of his, a Mr James Weatherby, was the first Keeper of the Match Book. Since 1773, the firm of Weatherby's have officially been the 'civil servants' of the Jockey Club. They also own and publish the Racing Calender and the General Stud Book.

After the formation of the Jockey Club, the great Classic races began to take shape. The oldest of the five British Classics is the St Leger, first run on Town Moor, Doncaster, in 1776. The race, which is open to 3-year-old colts and fillies, gets its name from a famous 18th-century sportsman, Lieutenant-general St Leger. It was first run over 2 miles (3.22 km) but changed in 1777 to its present distance of 1 mile 6½ furlongs (2.91 km). The first winner was a horse called Allabacullia.

Left: Simpatico, ridden by James Day, clears a fence during an American show jumping competition.
Right: British 3-day Event champion, Anneli Drummond-Hay, who transferred to international show jumping with the late Robert Hanson's brilliant horse Merely-A-Monarch. Anneli is now Mrs Errol Wucherphennig and lives in South Africa.

Above: A young cross-country rider sails out over a drop-fence on his good-looking grey horse.
Right: 1974 3-Day Event World Champion, American-born Bruce Davidson and Irish Cap go through the famous Trout Hatchery at Burghley.

The most important event in the British Racing Calendar is the Derby Stakes run on Epsom Downs each June for 3-year-old colts and fillies over a distance of 1 mile 4 furlongs (2.4 km). The race gets its name, which was decided by the toss of a coin with another of the turf's great patrons, Sir Charles Bunbury, from the 12th Earl of Derby. Ironically, it was Sir Charles' colt Diomed who won the first great race in 1780. The 2000 Guineas, the first of the classics each season is run at the Newmarket Spring meeting. It is run over a distance of 1 mile (1.6 km) for 3-year-old colts and fillies. It was first run in 1809 and won by a horse called Wizard. These three races make up the British Triple Crown and, although fillies are eligible, they tend to be beaten by the colts. The fillies have their own classics in the 1000 Guineas, also run at Newmarket and first contested in 1814, and the Oaks which was first run at Epsom in 1779.

The long history of British racing is full of famous owners such as the Lords Derby, the Earls of Sefton and Rosebery. There are also many great trainers such as John Scott (b. 1800s), Alec Taylor (b. 1862), Fred Darling (b. 1884), Sir Noel Murless (b. 1916) and Irish ace, Vincent O'Brien (b. 1917). Among the famous English jockeys feature Fred Archer (b. 1857) who was the first truly nationally-known race rider; Steve Donoghue (b. 1884) who rode 16 classic winners, Sir Gordon Richards (b. 1904) who became champion jockey 26 times and Lester Piggott (b. 1935), the most successful international jockey of all time. There were, of course many famous horses like Flying Childers, St Simon, Eclipse, Hyperion, Mahmoud, Bahram, Vaguely Noble, Ribot, Sea Bird, Brigadier Gerard, Grundy, Nijinsky, Mill Reef, Dahlia, Pawneese and The Minstrel, and many many more.

Racing in the USA was started by the early settlers and modelled on the British system. Between the end of the 17th and the 19th centuries, British Thoroughbreds were being imported to begin the long process of creating the American racehorse. Perhaps the most successful Thoroughbred in the world today.

The first recorded race meeting to take place in the USA was at Salisbury Plain, later known as Hemstead Plain, Long Island. Englishman Richard Nicolls, the first Governor of New York, offered a silver cup for a race to be run over the course in 1666. After the War of Independence, racing became more widespread throughout the country.

During the 1920s, politicians and community leaders became anxious about the malpractices of the bookmakers and racing promoters and the inter-track rivalry. General disgust with the racing fraternity brought considerable public support for anti-betting legislation. Along with the protective measures taken by British and French bloodstock breeders to keep American Thoroughbreds out of Europe, these laws brought the American racing and breeding industry almost to a halt. But, like so many events, these upheavals turned out, in the long run, to be the crossroads of the sport on the continent of America. It led to a State-run Tote Monopoly (Pari-Mutuel), Betting Boards, centralized racing and eventually to one of the most successful racing and breeding industries in the world today.

Thoroughbred racing is by far the most popular spectator sport in the USA. Some 50 million people go racing annually and the total value of stud farms, tracks and racehorses was recently valued at some 5 billion dollars. The three classic races that make up

Top left: Red-coated 'huntsmen' lead the post parade at Aqueduct, Long Island, New York.
Centre left: The field sweep round the long Tattenham Corner on Epsom Downs, England.
Bottom left: A field of American Pacers race for a good position down the back-stretch.
Above: Two English hurdle-racers leap the last hurdle before beginning the final sprint to the line.

the American triple crown are the Kentucky Derby, the Preakness Stakes and the Belmont Stakes, all open to three-year-olds only.

The Belmont Stakes is the senior of the American classics and Belmont Park, run by the New York Racing Association, is its home. The track is named after August Belmont a well-known banker and race-horse owner living at the turn of the century. It was opened in 1905, closed between 1911–12 due to the anti-betting laws, and re-opened in 1913 with the Pari-Mutuel installed. The Coaching Club American Oaks, the Acorn Stakes and the Mother Goose Stakes make up the 'Ladies' Triple Crown.

Churchill Downs in the heart of the Blue Grass Country is the home of the Kentucky Derby. The track with its oval shape and fast, level, dirt surface, is typical of the type raced on in the USA. The race was first run in 1875. Its present distance is $1\frac{1}{4}$ miles (2000 m). Since its first running, the race has been dominated by Kentucky-bred horses but in recent years the pattern has changed with the Californian-bred Swaps winning it in 1955 and the Canadian-bred Northern Dancer winning in 1964.

One of the oldest racetracks in the USA is Pimlico in the state of Maryland. This is the home of the Preakness Stakes, first run in 1873 and raced over a distance of $9\frac{1}{2}$ furlongs (1900 m). The race has suffered changes of distance, race-track and abandonment, but its roll of honour includes some of the greatest racehorses that the world has ever seen: Man O'War, Citation, Bold Ruler, Native Dancer, Northern Dancer and the multi-million dollar stallion, Secretariat.

Above: Hunting is one of the oldest equestrian sports. In Britain, some 200 packs hunt foxes from November to March. In many countries Drag-Hunting (a laid unnatural scent) has become the popular way to follow hounds.

The American racing scene has also produced some of the greatest riders too. Top-class jockeys such as Eddie 'Banana nose' Arcaro, English-born Johnny Longdon, Willie 'The Shoe' Shoemaker, rider of over 7000 winners, Canadian Sandy Hawley, and the latest young star of the 'silks' Steve Cauthen.

There are no regular classics in Australia, but each State has its own classic programme for 3-year-old colts and fillies. Most of the major races like the Melbourne Cup and Caufield Cup are run over distances ranging from 1½ miles to 2 miles (2400–3000 m). The bloodstock industries of New Zealand and Australia are so closely interwoven that whatever occurs in one country directly relates to the other. The Australian Stud Book was first published in 1878 and since those far off days, the Australasian-bred racehorse has become respected throughout the world for his toughness and ability.

There are some 700 race-tracks throughout Australia, but many of these are 'bush' tracks. It is at these 'bush' meetings that many of the future stars of Sydney, Melbourne, Brisbane, Adelaide and Perth racetracks, learn their craft. Australian jockeys, with their natural style and good judgement of pace have always been in demand all over the world. The late Rae Johnstone, who was based in Paris and rode for France's leading owner M. Marcel Boussac, rode the winners in practically every classic in Europe. The great George Moore and Bill Pyers carried on after Johnstone and in England men like Edgar Britt,

Willie Cook, Arthur 'Scobie' Breasley and Ron Hutchinson have successfully represented Australia.

## Show Jumping

The origins of show jumping, the most exacting of equestrian sports, are fairly obscure. In Britain, horse shows date back to the later part of the 18th century but these were mainly country fairs and agricultural shows. The horse events were mainly framed for working horses and young breeding stock.

The originators of the sport seem to be a mixture of soldier-riders of the great military riding academies who saw it as a sport and the horse-dealers, organizers of jumping events on the village green, who saw it as a very good way of selling their horses. It is likely that the horse-dealers were the first to take jumping seriously. They went jumping to prove how good their 'leaping' horses were, whereas the military rider, with his almost endless supply of mounts, was more interested in showing how good he was as a horseman, and how well trained his horse was.

From the outset, the aim of show jumping, in its simplest form, has always been to clear a series of unnatural obstacles. In show jumping we ask the horse to jump, accurately, a series of man-made fences set at calculated distances, within the confines of an indoor or outdoor arena. In dressage, we take advantage of many of the natural graces displayed by the horse; in racing and hunting we take advantage of the horse's instinctive spirit of competition within the herd. In

Left: A Driving Meet in England. The sport of driving now has its own National, European and World Championship meetings.
Above: Pony Trekking is the best way to enjoy the countryside.

show jumping, however, there are none of these natural stimulants. The fences are man-made and there is no herd from which to obtain security. These are the magic ingredients that make it such an exciting and satisfying sport.

The course and its fences are the basis of the sport, but it was not until after World War II, that the skill of the course-designer became truly recognized as an essential part of show jumping. Earlier it had been very much a makeshift affair; whosoever had the time and inclination would erect some jumps. But with the increase in popularity of the sport after the war it was soon realized that large audiences could be attracted to a horse show if it was entertaining. So the courses changed and the fences became more varied. More spread fences came into use, as did combinations of fences (doubles and trebles). Better groundlines and wings considerably changed show jumping techniques. Horses were better-trained and the more scientific rider came into his own. Course designers

themselves like Germany's Hans 'Mickey' Brinkmann; Britain's Pam Carruthers, ex-rider Alan Oliver, Jon Doney, and Alan Ball and Ireland's Eddie Taylor, became internationally known and respected.

Now the military influence has moved from the arena to the committee room. The civilian rider, professional and amateur, has come to the fore, and a business has grown up. The show jumping fraternity follow a somewhat nomadic life, travelling round the world with horses, grooms and trunks filled with equipment. Often they have six- to eight-horse trucks with a caravan hitched behind. Television encourages the sport. The colourful personalities of the show ring have a definite appeal to the viewers. Show jumpers live closely with a sport where disaster and success are twins and they are natural entertainers.

The first international show took place in Turin, Italy, in 1901. The Royal Dublin Society was founded in 1731 but it was not until 1868 that jumping became part of its programme.

1883 saw the birth of the great American international show at Madison Square Garden, New York. It started as a national show but in 1909 the President of the show, Alfred Vanderbilt, invited overseas competitors and the 'Garden' became one of the most

important international shows on the North American circuit, along with the Royal Winter Fair in Toronto, which was founded in 1925.

The Royal International Show, London, was first staged at Olympia in 1907. Then in the 1940s it moved to the White City before eventually settling in the indoor arena at the Empire Pool, Wembley, in North London. Wembley is also the venue of one of Britain's most popular international shows, The Horse of the Year Show.

The last decade has produced a brilliant crop of talented riders. To analyze their styles and successes would fill a book by itself. From Britain comes Peter Robeson, Olympic medalist and classical horseman, Harvey Smith perhaps the most popular show jumping rider the sport has ever seen, David Broome, ex-European and World Champion, Olympic Medalist and the finest natural horseman in the world, youngsters like Graham Fletcher, Rowland Fernyhough and Debbie Johnsey. One must also include National Champion, Caroline Bradley and Olympic Silver Medalist, Marion Mould. From Germany comes

multiple Olympic Medalists Hans Gunter Winkler, Fritz Ligges and the now retired Montreal Olympic Gold Medalist Alwin Schockemöhle. From France come Pierre Jonquères d'Oriola, Hubert Parot, Janou Tissot and Christophe Cuyer. From Belgium come the European team champions, the tall, blond-haired Johan Heins, holder of the 1977 Individual European title and from Ireland the exciting rider, Eddie Macken. Australia provide John Fahey, and Art Uytendaal—winner of four major contests at the 1977 Royal Melbourne Show on his jumper Tongala, and neighbouring New Zealand gives us Harvey Wilson and John Cottle. The 'new' American crowd-pullers, like the red-headed Rodney Jenkins with his relaxed, flowing, but accurate style. Michael Matz, William 'Buddy' Brown, and Dennis Murphy are all a force to be reckoned with under the brilliant guidance of United States Equestrian team coach Bertalan de Nemethy. From Canada comes John Simpson, from Italy, the home of modern equitation, comes another ex-World Champion Graziano Mancinelli and the veteran d'Inzeo brothers, Raimondo and Piero. From

Far left: Competitors trot through Cougar Park in the USA Trevis Cup ride. Some 100 miles are covered in one day.
Left: America is the traditional home of Western riding. Here are four riders in Western dress. Stirrups are longer on the high Western Saddles giving the rider a straighter leg which is a comfortable position for a long day in the saddle. The horses are schooled to go on a light rein and to neck-rein.

Brazil, but now French-based, comes one of the most pleasing horsemen to watch, Nelson Pessoa.

Horses, too, have become personalities in this great international sport. With unforgettable, legendary names like Britain's Foxhunter, Tosca, Prince Hal, Sunsalve, Red Admiral, Moxy and Pennwood Forge Mill; Germany's Meteor, Simona, Donald Rex; America's Untouchable, Nautical, Czar d'Esprit, Tomboy, Sinbad and Idle Dice.

### Eventing

Combined training, also known as 3-day eventing and horse-trialing, comes from the era of the great military academies in the days of cavalry and horse-transport. The famous schools of Saumur and Fontainebleau in France, Pinerolo in Italy, Madrid in Spain, West Point in the USA and Weedon in England all contributed to this sport which is tough, demanding and growing in popularity.

The competition is basically divided into three phases: dressage, an obedience test, then a speed and endurance course. This is usually made up of the roads and tracks, steeplechase and cross-country obstacles. And finally, a test of soundness and ability to continue after the tough cross-country section—the show jumping phase. Riders tackle a course of smallish, coloured fences within the confines of an arena. Between each phase the horses are subjected to a stiff veterinary examination to prevent a courageous and willing horse being asked to do too much.

The event takes place over three days in senior competitions like Badminton and Burghley in England, Fontainebleau in France and Ledyard Farm in the USA. It is scaled down to only one or two days in the novice and intermediate divisions.

Concours Complet, as it is known on the continent, has been part of the three equestrian events in the Olympic Games since it was first added to the modern programme in 1912. It has been a very popular sport on the continent of Europe for many years but when Great Britain entered a team in the 1936 Games, the event did not even exist in England. Since then Britain has made up for lost time by becoming one of the leading 'Eventing' nations.

73

The history of the sport is full of stories of men, women and horses battling against injury and the elements. The riders who competed in the Mexico Olympics in 1968 must hold the record for determination in the face of adversity. In a monsoon-type storm, the British team, led by 54-year-old Major Derek Allhusen, won the Gold medal, with the American team finishing second and the Australians finishing third. The new stars of the game in Britain are players like the attractive and energetic Lucinda Prior-Palmer, three times European Champion and the serious, dedicated Captain Mark Phillips.

In 1960, 73 riders from 19 nations arrived in Rome for the Olympics, where the cross-country course was one of the toughest and most sensational ever seen. In that year, one of the finest event teams in the history of the sport arrived on the scene, the Gold-medal-winning Australian team of Laurie Morgan, Neale Lavis and Bill Roycroft, riding Salad Days, Mirrabooka and Our Solo. The Australians are natural horsemen, they believe in giving their horses as much freedom as they can, and in getting them exceptionally fit.

One final, outstanding success-story that must be included is that of the American team with 1974 World Champion Bruce Davidson. They won the team World Championship title at Burghley in 1974 and the individual Gold medal.

In France, England, America and Australia young riders with ability are now coming to the fore, with television coverage bringing a wider audience that appreciates the technicalities of the sport. This is very encouraging, not only for the sport and its promoters, but also for the future of the cross-country horse.

**Dressage**
Dressage, in the modern sense, is the basis of all equitation. Whether the horse is going to be a jumper, a hunter or just an ordinary riding horse, some form of dressage training must be given to encourage the horse to carry a rider in a balanced and comfortable manner.

The domesticated horse develops in the same way as he would in the wild, but for him it is Man and not nature who will determine his growth and development. This is the object of dressage: to substitute a system of training that will bring the horse to physical and mental maturity as nature does with the horse of the prairies or the steppes.

Dressage, however, once the mysterious art of the

Left: Calf roping at a rodeo. Notice how the cowboy uses the horn of his western saddle to secure the steer.
Top right: Bronco riding is one of the biggest spectator sports in America, Canada and Australia. This bronc has just plunged out of the chute and is going well. The buckeroo must keep one hand above his shoulder line and stay on the wild, bucking bronc for more than 10 seconds. Some broncs are famous for their skill in being able to unseat their rider, time and time again. There are also star riders of the rodeo, who like the pop-stars, get sacks of fan mail each week.

straight line, two-track and half-pass work, piaffes and passage. These are all performed at the natural collected paces and the extended gaits. In dressage, 'extended' does not mean going faster as in racing. It refers to the extension of the stride without loss of balance and without quickening as in the extended walk and trot.

Dressage is more of a European sport than an American one, but its following is increasing each year and, although still a minority sport, some of the riders and horses, particularly at Grand Prix level, are beginning to emerge as 'stars'. People are taking more interest in the art of classical equitation and this has led to an enthusiastic understanding of dressage, its demands and its execution.

### Steeplechasing

The sport of steeplechasing came from the English hunting field. Although many countries stage hurdle-racing, steeplechasing or hunt racing at a national level, it has remained a particularly English sport.

In 18th-century England, the favourite sport of the county gentry was to race in a wagered match from one village steeple to the steeple of a neighbouring village, across natural country, jumping natural obstacles. This was the early form of steeplechasing and hunt racing which quickly spread all over England. The first record of such a match was in 1752 run over $4\frac{1}{2}$ miles (about 7200 m) in Ireland. The course was set from Buttevant Church to the spire of St Leger Church. The first match involving more than two horses, in this case three, was held in Leicestershire, the heart of the British midlands, in 1792.

In 1810, the first real steeplechase was run over a planned course, just outside the English county town of Bedford. Eight fences had to be jumped over a distance of 3 miles (about 4800 m) and the race was run in heats. The winner was Mr Spencer's jumper, Fugitive. The first meeting for steeplechase races was organized near St Albans, Hertfordshire, in the year 1830. Since those exciting days the sport, under the control of the National Hunt Committee and the Jockey Club, has become the 'winter' game of British race-fans. The Anglo-Irish steeplechaser has become a sort of sub-breed to the flat-racing Thoroughbred.

The greatest steeplechase in the world is, without doubt, the Grand National run at Aintree on the out-skirts of Liverpool, in northern England. It is run over a course just over 4 miles (6 kms). There are 30 gorse-type fences on this, the toughest course in the world, including Bechers Brook, named after the famous amateur rider Capt. Becher, Valentines Brook, the Canal Turn and the Chair. The race was first run in 1837 and the present idol of the British jumping fans is Mr Nöel le Mare's Red Rum, three times winner of this race and twice runner-up, a record yet to be beaten or equalled.

classical schools, is now also a competitive sport and forms part of the Olympic competition. It has its own 'Derby' at Hickstead in England, and at Hamburg, West Germany. Each year, riders converge on these two centres, and the big championships staged at Aachen, Germany, and Goodwood, England, from all over the world. Competition is fierce while material rewards are, as yet, small. Now and again someone may sell a 'Prix St Georges' horse for a large sum of money, but this is very rare. Dressage riders spend a great deal of time 'making' their horses, so once they have reached international level they tend to keep them.

A Grand Prix or Championship competition is long and complicated. It is a test of the horse's education. There are movements on the turn, on the circle, on the

Left: Steer Wrestling at the Rodeo. The cowboy lines up his steer then leaps from the saddle and brings his steer to the ground for roping.
Below right: Spectacle at the rodeo. An 'Indian' shows off a traditional costume. The word rodeo comes from the Spanish word, 'rodear', meaning to go round. Originally it was a term given to the round-up of cattle on the American prairies but it soon became used to name the shows where cowboys and cowponies exhibited the skill of their work.

The USA also has a Grand National, run at Belmont Park. America's most famous race over obstacles is the Maryland Hunt Cup, better known as the timber 'classic'. The race was first run in 1894 as a competition between the members of the Elkridge Hunt and the Green Valley Hunt. It was restricted to amateur riders at first, but now professionals can ride in the race. The course at Glyndon, Maryland, covers 4 miles with 22 post and rail fences. Many crack American jump-riders of the 20th century have made their names over the course. D. Michael Smithwick has won it six times and Tommy Crompton Smith has taken the laurels on no less than five occasions. One of America's greatest steeplechasers was Jay Trump. Tommy Crompton Smith found him in a small yard in a shanty town and bought him for $2000 on behalf of Mrs Stephenson of Ohio. Jay Trump, with little or no credentials, left the 'gyp' stables of Charles Town, West Virginia, to seek fame and fortune on the jumping tracks of Maryland, Aintree, and Paris, before returning to Maryland for a last honourable triumph.

New Zealand has produced many top steeplechasers in recent years including the tough horse, Grand Canyon trained in Britain by Derek Kent and ridden by Irishman, Ron Barry. Grand Canyon won the 1976 Colonial Cup run at Camden, North Carolina.

### Trotting and Pacing
Looking back to the ancient Egyptians, Greeks and Romans, there is plenty of evidence to show where the sport of racing trotting horses came from. Chariot-racing, the forerunner of this exciting sport, was an every day happening. When not warring or hunting, horses and chariots would be taken to the local arena for a day's racing. These affairs were pretty rough,

competition was fierce and it was not unusual for horses and drivers to be involved in dramatic crashes and fatal accidents.

It was in rural England, in the days before mechanized transport, that the sport re-appeared. Crowds flocked to country fairs to see the trotting races. The light carriage was a common sight on the unmade, bumpy roads of the counties of Norfolk and Suffolk. Tradesmen and farmers all kept fine 'framed' horses, in the same way that the average family today keeps an automobile. These horses began to be used for business and communication and competition soon crept in. Who could deliver the quickest? Who had the best trotting horses? So, like racing, the 'matching' of trotters was born. The Ambler became known as a type of driving horse. Surprisingly, the sport is not popular in modern Britain but in Europe, Africa, the Americas, Australia and New Zealand, trotting and pacing are leading spectator sports.

The Norfolk Trotter and Roadster were introduced into the USA and, after a number of years of crossing Thoroughbred blood, the Standardbred or American Trotter was born. This is a horse of heart and stamina that can run heat after heat at top speed without tiring.

The difference between the Pacer and the Trotter is in the action. The Pacer is trained to run with a lateral action, i.e. near-fore, near-hind, off-fore, off-hind, whereas the Trotter uses the natural diagonal action of near-fore, off-hind, off-fore, near-hind.

Harness Racing today, especially in America, Australia and New Zealand, is big business, with meetings being held in luxurious stadiums, often at night under floodlights.

### Rodeos
There are, of course, endless pastimes and sports

one can enjoy with the horse and pony. Fortunately, many of them are enjoyed by horses and ponies too, such as hunting, the oldest of equestrian sports. Rodeo is a magic word that conjures up the spirit of America and the Australian outback. The everyday life of the gauchos and cowboys, rounding up cattle, driving herds of horses, breaking in new ones for their work, was hard and lonely. They would often argue about the virtues of the Galvayne or Rarey systems for breaking wild horses. Each rider would claim to be the best horsebreaker in the outfit or the fastest at cutting and roping a steer. Man's need to master the animal kingdom and to show himself superior to his colleagues soon turned the cowboys' skills into 'competition' events.

Sydney Galvayne was a celebrated, 19th century horsebreaker and trainer. His theory was to use the great strength of the horse against himself and he boasted of never having a failure. He went to England in 1884 to lecture on his techniques, and in 1887 appeared before Queen Victoria. John Solomon Rarey (1827–1886) was a farmer and horse tamer from Ohio. His method was to exhaust the horse before starting to 'work' him or 're-make' him. Although the Rarey system is the better known of the two, the Galvayne

method is accepted as more humane.

The State Fair became the mecca for the buckeroos in search of fame and fortune; bronco-busting was part of the festival and the public loved it. Gradually, however, the jeep, the helicopter, and the estate wagon, with their radio telephones, took over from the horse. The rodeo then joined the commercial ranks of the entertainment industry. The great Western spectacle, based on the earlier daily life of the cowboy, is now America's second largest equestrian spectator-sport after flat-racing.

One looks back to the pioneering spirit of the founding fathers and the freedom of vast plains and land masses where wild horses roamed and men carved out new communities. Trail-Riding, or Long Distance riding as it is also known, is one of the most natural of horse-sports and now enjoys a large following of equestrian enthusiasts across the continents of America, Australia and Europe.

# Horses in art

Art is Man's conception of what he feels, sees and what he hopes to see. Since he first took shelter in caves and made himself a home, Man seems to have been fascinated by the horse. Numerous prehistoric cave paintings have been discovered featuring powerful images of the horse. At first it was an animal to be hunted, later the horse became a symbol of ritual and mystical overtones. Finally when domesticated, he became a friend and servant.

Gradually the artistic images of horses became more elaborate, more suggestive of magic and religion and hunting ritual in the New Stone Age. This we can see from the fascinating cave-drawings found in the Grotte de Lascaux in France, at Altamira in Spain and on the walls of the mountain homes of the upper regions of the Hautes-Pyrénées and at Schaffhouse in Switzerland.

The ancient Egyptians, Urartians and Assyrians left behind their bas-relief depicting lion hunts using horse-drawn chariots; of warriors launching spears or firing a form of bow and arrow on horse-back or driven in chariots. The pre-history Chinese and Indian

**Left: A Chinese glazed figurine that can be seen in the Victoria and Albert Museum, London. One of the fascinations of this type of figure is the accuracy and detail achieved by the Chinese artist.**
**Right: A battle scene on an ancient Greek vase shows a mounted Amazon battling with a warrior.**

Far right: A stylized statuette of the Roman Imperial period, possibly a portrait of Alexander the Great and his mount Bucephalus. Looking at the scale of the horseman, particularly the position of his lower leg, it appears that the horse was quite small.

Right: A Greek vase depicting a horse-race. Here the riders look small and light while the stallions seem large, rangy and finely-bred. It is interesting that, although the bridles are fairly advanced in design, the riders have no saddle and stirrups. The Greeks and Romans often used a blanket secured by a girth, and many horseman used to tuck their feet into the girth.

Below: Here is another Greek vase, beautifully decorated, depicting a completely different type of horse being used in chariots. These horses are smaller-boned but finely bred with beautifully-shaped heads.

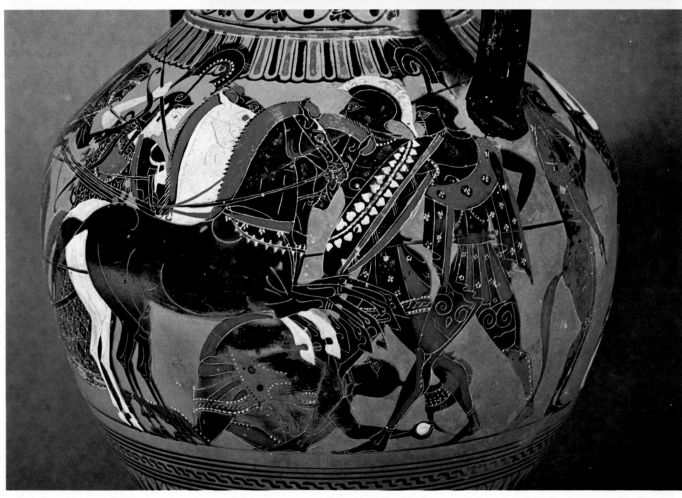

Emperors immortalized the horse in statues, statuettes and figurines cast in rare and priceless stone and metals.

The nomadic peoples and the so-called barbarians left, along their trading routes, fine examples of their ornaments, costumes, shields, swords, drinking and cooking utensils, all of great beauty and craftsmanship. The style is perhaps more aggressive than that of the educated peoples, but then these artists lived in an aggressive world, the world of the elements, the world of nature.

The classical Greeks rode and drove horses and liked to be portrayed astride fine-boned, muscular steeds. But, in fact, much of their sculpture and painting contained a fair amount of artistic licence. In ancient Greece, the horse was a rare animal, both expensive and exotic. In the busy streets of Athens it was quite an unusual occurrence to see a horse ridden or driven.

Ancient Greece had not been the home of horses since the days of Neanderthal man, being rocky, mountainous and poor in pasture. Nevertheless, there was one region where horse-breeding was carried out. This was on the fertile plains of Thessaly. In fact, Alexander the Great's favourite horse Bucephalus was said to be Thessalian-bred. It appears, however, that the major part of the labour force and the foundation stock were imported. Horses were only available to the very rich and became a symbol of rank and social status.

It was, therefore, the Greeks and the Romans that exploited the artistic image of the horse for prestige. A tradition that followed on in the Renaissance period, the age of chivalry and honour. For during this time, the artist portrayed subjects which he knew would please his patron. The artist had to project his master in an heroic and noble style like in Paolo Uccello's great Italian war-horse, one of the battle-pieces commissioned by Piero de Medici to commemorate the skirmish of San Romano in April 1432.

So when looking at equestrian art, or any other art for that matter, one must make allowances for the artists' licence often contrived to please wealthy patrons. It was not, however, until the 17th and 18th centuries that Europe experienced a surge of interest in equestrian art. The poses and action shots look strange to us today because the camera was yet to prove that the horse does not gallop with his four legs spread-eagled from each corner of his body. By studying paintings of this period that we are shown a graphic account of life, horses and occasions that are fascinating to know and to look at.

It is difficult to know where to start as there is so much to choose from, but the earliest artist of the British sporting school was Francis Barlow (c. 1626–1702). Barlow worked in London as an etcher besides

being a painter of English country scenes. Many of his fine pictures can be seen at Clandon Park, Guildford in southern England. After Barlow came one of the great painters, John Wootton (*c*. 1677–1765). This talented painter, who studied under Jan Wyck, the Dutch-born artist, and also in Italy, was a master of the large canvas. He was patronized by the Second Duke of Beaufort, one of England's most famous hunting families. Wootton specialized in hunting scenes, landscapes, battles and portraits of the race-horses of the day. His massive canvases can be seen in many stately homes like Althorp in the Midlands and Longleat in the West.

In 1700, John Sartorius Senior was born, destined to found a dynasty of sporting artists. He was the son of a Nuremburg engraver and it is thought that he became established in England in or around 1720. He had a somewhat stiff style unlike the smooth, flowing classical style of so many British equestrian artists, but he painted portraits of several racehorses for influential owners working to the English approach to sporting art. He died in 1780. John Sartorius's son Francis (1734–1804) gained wider recognition than his father but having been taught by him, tended to follow the same limited style. Francis painted many match-races, hunters and racehorses including several

portraits of the immortal Eclipse. John Nost Sartorius (1759–1828) was the son of Francis and perhaps the most talented of the three artists. Many prints were made of his works and one of his sons, John Francis was a successful sporting artist.

John Frederick Herring senior (1795–1865) started out his career as a stage-coachman on the Doncaster–Halifax route. He taught himself to paint before going to study under Abraham Cooper RA (1787–1868). He was a prolific worker, painting the portraits, in a rather undramatic style, of 33 consecutive St Leger winners and 18 Derby winners. But his work was very popular and he eventually retired to Tonbridge in south eastern England to paint very precise but attractive farmyard scenes. His sons, John Frederick Junior, Charles and Ben followed in his footsteps although their talent was limited. Their work was often confused with that of their father.

Even more confusion arises when studying the work of one of Britain's most famous families of sporting artists, the Alkens. Henry Thomas Alken Senior (1785–1851) was the most talented member of the family. He was born in Soho, London, far from the Leicestershire hunting scenes that he was to be renowned for. He worked in both oils and water-colours and illustrated several successful sporting

Left: The 13th-century bronze horses of St Mark's in Venice.
Above: The Byerley Turk, one of the founding stallions of the modern Thoroughbred, painted in the typical style of the 17th-century sporting artist.

books. Samuel Alken (1756–1815) was the senior member of the family and uncle to Henry Alken Senior. But the artist who caused most confusion was Henry Samuel Alken (1810–1894), the Ipswich-born son of Henry Senior. He, too, painted sporting subjects but with slightly less talent and had the annoying habit of deliberately using the same signature, 'H. Alken' or 'H.A.'.

One of the most widely reproduced paintings in equestrian art was Marie Rosalie (Rosa) Bonheur's (1822–1899) *The Horse Fair*, first shown at the Paris Exhibition in 1855. Another of her celebrated works was *The Duel*, a dramatic painting of two stallions, Hobgoblin and The Godolphin Arabian fighting for the favours of the mare Roxana.

The three great classic painters of British sporting art are George Stubbs, Alfred Munnings and Lionel Edwards. Their works today are as in demand and coveted as any 'Old Master'. George Stubbs, RA (1724–1806) was the son of a Liverpool currier and had very little training in his chosen art. He first made a living out of portrait painting but soon became obsessed with the anatomy of the horse. In 1758, in a bleak Lincolnshire farmhouse he dissected horse carcases to learn more of his subject. In 1766 he published, with his own engravings, the book which was to become a classic, *The Anatomy of the Horse*. His portraits of famous racehorses of the day were brilliant but his pastoral series, *Mares and Foals*, are masterpieces.

Sir Alfred James Munnings, KCVO, PRA (1878–1959) was an equestrian artist of outstanding ability and immense popularity. His fluent and vivid pictures

Above: An early print of North American Indians mounted on mustangs during a buffalo hunt.

of the modern Thoroughbred are unequalled to this day.

Over in North America, a new breed of contemporary artists arose, inspired by the brash, harsh, exciting world of vast plains, wild mustangs, the indian and the cowboy. These were folk-painters and on-the-spot-reporters like Charles Russell, Frederic Remington, Catlin, Koerner and Walker.

Charles Russell, was a frontiersman and knew the people and places which he painted. After an unremarkable career at school he went to an art school in St Louis only to leave after three days. At the age of 16, a friend of the family, 'Pike' Miller gave him a job tending sheep on the Judith Basin, Montana.

Young Russell lived on the ranch for about a year making sketches, losing sheep and eventually getting himself fired. He then spent a winter with the Blackfeet Indians before a hunter called Jake Hoover took pity on him and offered him shelter. Charlie stayed a year in Jake's cabin drawing the wild, raw world around him. Then fate was to offer him a job which he could master when he was hired as a horse-wrangler for a cattle roundup. Charlie was very successful and spent the next 11 years working as a wrangler, cowpuncher and ranch hand. And all the time throughout this period he continued to draw, sketch and paint. The cowboys, themselves, liked his work. His pictures were good and they were accurate. The cowboys could recognize at a glance a certain horse or a well-known character, and they liked it. In 1893 Charlie moved to Great Falls, Montana, and became a full-time painter selling his work to friends or in Sid Willis's Mint Bar for $25!

Then Russell met and married Kentucky-born Nancy Cooper. Although only a teenager at the time, Nancy became Charlie's astute manager finding more buyers for his works and getting him far better prices. In 1911 Charlie's first one-man show was held in New York. The wrangler and cowhand from St Louis became a national celebrity. His paintings, as clear as the eye of the camera, live on to tell us the true stories of the Wild West and the men and horses that went into the unknown to create one of the best known, best loved legends in the history of modern man, the cowboy and his horse.

**Two brilliant American artists who realistically captured the spirit of the West.**
**Right: 'A dash for timber' by Frederic Remington.**
**Below: 'Wild Horse Hunters' by ex-cowboy Charles Russell.**

# Care of the horse

## Handling Horses

Understanding the horse's mentality and having sympathy with him are essential for successful handling. The horse, as a creature of habit, likes routine. Feed times, for example, should not vary; 'riding-out' should be at the same time each morning.

Always approach a horse's shoulder, whether he is in a field or in the stable. Walk quietly up to him and when you are near enough, pat or stroke the lower neck and shoulder and speak to him. To lead a horse that is not familiar to you, approach and handle him from the near-side (left), as most horses are used to being handled from this side. Place your right hand, back uppermost, on the rope or reins, near the head-collar or bridle. The slack of the rope or reins should be gathered up in the left hand. Never twist the reins or rope around the left hand, as if the horse jumps away from you or shies, you could be dragged along the ground and injured.

## Stables

The loose box is the best form of stabling, as it allows greater freedom for the horse. The box should measure 4.2 m × 3.7 m (14 ft × 12 ft) for a horse, and 3.7 m × 3 m (12 ft × 10 ft) for an average pony. The door should be at least 1.2 m (4 ft) wide and high enough to allow the animal to pass in and out without having to lower his head. There must be absolutely no danger of him hitting his head. The door should be in two halves, the bottom half equipped with double bolts. Horses like to see what is going on around them so the top half of the door should remain open.

The floor must be 'warm' (concrete, for example, is 'cold'), and non-slippery. It should be sloped towards the door for drainage purposes. The box must be well-ventilated, light and airy. Horses and ponies should not be kept in dark or damp stables otherwise their health will suffer.

Left: Looking after a pony is part of the fun of owning it. This young girl is 'picking-out' her pony's feet, a job that must be done regularly. There are two systems of shoeing, hot-shoeing and cold-shoeing. In hot-shoeing the shoe is specially made to fit the foot, then it is tried for fitting so that corrections can be made before it is finally cooled and nailed into position. In cold-shoeing a ready-made shoe is altered to fit the foot as accurately as possible.
Right: Shovel, fork, brush, bucket and wheelbarrow are essential equipment for keeping the loose box and stable yard clean.

## Bedding

Straw is generally accepted as the best bedding material for horses. It is warm and comfortable underfoot, and has the added advantage that it can be banked up around the walls and door to keep out draughts. Wheat straw is the best. It is easy to handle, permits free drainage and is warm and bright in appearance. Barley straw tends to be rough and can irritate the skin but barley straw from a combine harvester is finer and makes good bedding. Oat straw can be used, but great care must be taken because the horse (especially a pony) will have a tendency to eat it. This can cause minor ailments such as colic.

Shavings and sawdust used together or separately, make a cheap form of bedding. They are very useful materials for horses that tend to eat their bedding. If used together, sawdust should be used for the underlayer. Maintenance, however, is difficult, and the nature of the material does not allow good drainage.

Stables should be 'mucked out' daily, and the bedding material replenished with fresh. Throughout the working day, any droppings should be removed regularly. Clean stabling and yards are an indication of good stable management and the mark of a true horseman.

## Grooming

The objectives of grooming ('strapping' is the term used in professional stables) are to promote health; to maintain condition; to prevent disease (particularly

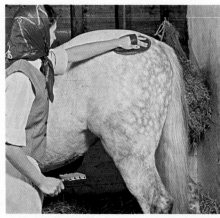

Far left: Mucking-out is an important part of stable routine and important to the health of the stabled horse.
Near left: Use of the body brush and curry comb. After every third or fourth stroke of the body brush, the curry comb is used to clean out the brush.
Below: This stabled horse is well-rugged up, smart and clean, and ready to relax at the end of the day.
Right: Here the farrier is shoeing a foot.

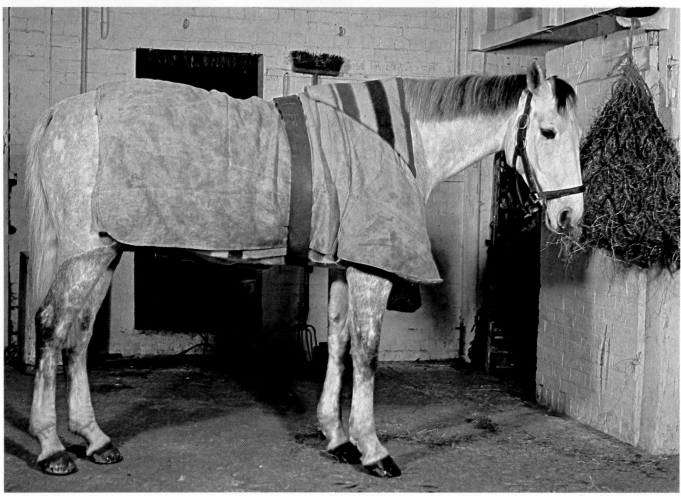

skin troubles); to ensure cleanliness; and to improve appearance. To groom correctly, a grooming kit is necessary.

Use a *hoof pick* for cleaning out the feet.

A *dandy brush* is used for taking off heavy dirt, caked mud and dust. It is very useful for grooming a grass-kept pony.

The *body brush* is used for removing dust and scurf in the coat, mane and tail.

The *curry comb*, which is made of metal or india rubber, is *only* used for cleaning the body brush. The metal variety should not be used directly on the horse's body.

A *water brush* is used to damp down the mane and tail and can be used for washing the feet.

Use a *stable sponge* for cleaning the eyes, nostrils and dock.

A *wisp* (which must be made by an expert from soft hay or straw) is used for massaging and promoting circulation. It should not be used by an inexperienced person.

A *stable rubber* is a linen cloth used for final rubbing down after strapping.

## Feeding the stabled horse

The stabled horse should be fed little and often on clean, good quality food. Give the horse plenty of bulk food such as hay. This simulates natural grazing as the digestive organs are always well-filled. Without adequate bulk, the digestive process will not remain well-balanced. Do not suddenly change your horse's diet. All changes should be gradual, spread over several days. It is extremely important to keep to the same daily feeding times.

Feed the horse according to the amount of work which he is doing. Increase the amount of concentrated foods, such as oats, when the horse is doing hard work and decrease accordingly when he is only working lightly. Do not feed concentrates if the horse is sick or not working, but increase the bulk. Do not make your horse do any hard work after a large feed or when the stomach is full of grass.

Do not give water to a horse directly after he has had a large feed. Give water before feeding as this aids digestion. If a supply of water is normally kept in the box, the horse may take a drink during or after feeding, but this will do no harm as it will not be a long draught. Always keep some rock salt in the manger, or put a small amount of salt in the feed. This will ensure that the horse drinks regularly so that undigested food is washed out of the stomach.

## Concentrated foods

*Oats.* These are a balanced, nutritious and readily-digested food. They can be fed either whole, bruised or boiled. In order to maintain the protein, oats should

Left: The grass-kept horse must have clean, fresh water available to him at all times.
Right: A race-horse trainer out with his string on a frosty winter's morning. Regular exercise is essential to the health and happiness of the stabled horse. Plenty of walking, trotting and steady cantering will prepare him for faster work or jumping. One should start with short distances or small obstacles to build up to complete fitness and suppleness. The racehorse or competition horse is an athlete, so his mind and body must be brought to a 'peak' at just the right time.

not be over-crushed. Do not feed 'dusty' oats. Oats are an energy-producing food so careful attention must be paid when feeding them to very small ponies as they can become too lively.

*Barley and flaked maize.* These are used in many countries, with success. But care must be taken when feeding flaked maize as it has a tendency to overheat the blood. Barley, if boiled, is a good pick-me-up for tired or sick horses.

*Beans.* A very nutritious food but, like maize, are 'heating'. Only small quantities should be given to ponies, and they should be bruised or split.

*Horse and Pony cubes.* These are man-made, compound concentrates popular with some horse- and pony-owners today. They are labour saving (saving on storage and mixing, for example) but they are comparatively expensive and are of no great advantage when training quality horses for competition and racing. Most cubes are made from oats, bran, maize, barley, locust bean, linseed cake, groundnut meal, grass meal and molasses, plus vitamins and minerals. They should be fed mixed with bran or chaff at the following rate: 454–680 g (1–1½ lb) of cubes replacing 454 g (1 lb) of oats.

## Bulk foods

The two main bulk foods natural to the horse are grass and hay. The pony or horse kept on grass obviously feeds himself, but grass management must be good. 'Sick' land will produce poorly-conditioned horses. The grass should be even over all the pasture, succulent and well-coloured; it should not be tufty or weedy. Fresh water or a running stream should be in the paddock. An open-fronted shelter should be provided for protection in the winter and for shade in the summer. Horses should be moved from one paddock to another to ensure balanced feeding, and the 'resting' paddocks should be rolled and chain-harrowed regularly. The droppings of horses and ponies out at grass must be raked and spread every day.

For the stabled horse, hay is a good substitute for grass. This should be sweet-smelling and fibrous. Four varieties are best for horses; sainfoin (the most nutritious), clover, mixture and meadow. Clover hay is rich but must be of the very best quality; the poorer grades tend to become dusty and mouldy. Mixture hay (rye grass, clovers and trefoil) makes a good, general-purpose bulk feed. Meadow hay is of poor food-value but if it is not too low in quality it makes a

Above: Mares and foals out at grass on a stud farm. Young bloodstock are best kept under the combined system of grazing during the day and then coming into the stable for the night.

good bulk feed for roughed-off horses. New hay (less than six months old) should never be fed to horses or ponies. Chaff (chopped hay) should only be made from better-grade hay. Oat straw made into chaff is often a good bulk substitute for heavy horses.

## Other feeding stuffs

*Bran.* This gives bulk to the oat ration and, when fed damp as a bran mash, has laxative properties. It is very good for sick horses or those suddenly taken out of work through, for instance, injury. A bran mash should be fed to the stabled horse at least once a week. To make a bran mash, fill a stable bucket about two-thirds full of bran, pour on boiling water and mix thoroughly until really wet. Cover the mixture with a sack and allow it to stand until cool enough to feed. The end-product should be 'crumble-dry'. A little salt should be added.

*Linseed.* This improves condition and gives a gloss to the coat. Very good for ponies living out in winter, it can be fed as a 'jelly' or as a 'tea'. The daily allowance should not exceed 454 g (1 lb), before cooking, for horses and 227 g (0.5 lb) for small ponies. To make linseed jelly, place a handful of linseed in a saucepan, cover it with water and allow it to soak (with the lid on) overnight. The following evening, add more water and bring it to the boil. This is important as unboiled linseed can be poisonous. Allow the mixture to cool. If it has been properly made, it should set like a jelly. Mix it in with an evening feed, in small quantities. To make linseed tea, prepare as for jelly but add more water. The water in which the linseed is boiled is very nutritious. Bran can be added to make a linseed mash.

*Gruel.* A very good pick-me-up for a tired horse. Put two handfuls of oatmeal into a bucket, pour on boiling water and stir well. Allow to cool. The gruel must be thin enough for the horse to be able to drink it.

*Dried sugar beet pulp.* This should be soaked for a period, and must not be fed dry. It is a good bulk food for horses that are 'roughed-off', but has very low food-value content.

*Molasses.* A by-product of sugar manufacturing processes, it is nutritious and palatable. It should be thinned down with warm water, and then sprinkled on food. It must not be used for making low quality feed more tempting. It is very useful for encouraging a 'fussy' feeder.

*Root crops.* Carrots, swedes, turnips, beetroots and parsnips, can add variety to feeds. They must be well scrubbed in warm water and sliced into fingers. They should never be given chopped, as there is a danger of them sticking in the throat and causing choking.

## The healthy horse

The head is alert with bright wide-open eyes that are interested in their surroundings. The ears constantly move backwards and forwards alertly. The inside

Left: Ponies love company, although the one shown here seems intent on eating his companion's jersey as well as the proffered hay.
Above: A show pony relaxes in his trailer. He has been tied-up with just enough length of rope to give him freedom and comfort. He has a full hay-net to munch on and with the side- and rear-ramp down, he can look around and enjoy a steady flow of fresh air. This pony is particularly lucky as he has a friend to keep him company.

lining of the eyes (this can be pulled down gently with the fingers) and nostrils is salmon-pink in colour. The horse should eat all his feeds and drink regularly and the coat should be smooth and glossy. You should be able to slide the skin easily over the ribs.

The horse should stand evenly on all four feet. Occasionally horses rest a hind-leg and this is normal and natural, but if a fore-leg is rested, this is a sign that the leg or shoulder is bothering the horse.

Droppings, passed about eight times a day, are formed into balls that break on hitting the ground. Urine, which is thick and light yellow in colour, is passed several times a day. This is known as 'staling'. The normal temperature of a horse is 38°C (100.5°F). The normal respiratory rate is 10–12 to the minute.

## Veterinary notes

You should keep a medicine cabinet easily accessible in the yard or in your home. It must be kept clean and dust-free, and out of reach of children. A first-aid box should include the following:

A veterinary clinical thermometer; a pair of 4 in (10 cm) blunt pointed surgical scissors; calico bandages, 2 in (5 cm) and 3 in (7.5 cm) sizes; several 2 oz (57 g) rolls of cotton wool (the larger rolls are unsuitable as the unused portions, once opened, tend to become soiled and unfit for use); a few 1 oz (28 g) packets of lint; a roll of 'gamgee' tissue; small packets of oiled silk or mackintosh; two colic drinks from your own veterinary surgeon; a pint (0.6 litre) bottle of lead lotion; a bottle of veterinary embrocation; a bottle of witch-hazel lotion; a 1 lb (454 g) tin of kaolin paste; a jar of cough electuary; a tin of antibiotic dusting powder (with soft cloth as a duster); a jar of common salt, salt tablets or Epsom salts; a bottle of glycerine. N.B. Do not attempt to use the thermometer until you have been instructed in its use by a veterinary surgeon.

## First aid

*Wound dressing.* The use of antiseptics and disinfectants can cause damage to injured tissues and with modern antibiotics they are not needed. Clean wounds with a saline solution and then apply an antibiotic provided by your veterinary surgeon.

*Poulticing.* Epsom salts and glycerine made into a paste is simple and efficient. Kaolin paste is the best for treating bruising, abscess-formation, swelling and pain. Take the lid off the tin, place the tin in a saucepan half-full of water and boil for five minutes. Test the temperature of the paste on the back of the hand before applying to the injured area. Apply thickly using a flat piece of metal (an old blunt kitchen knife will do the job). Then cover with lint or cotton wool. Wrap a sheet of oiled silk or mackintosh over the dressing, then bandage loosely with a woollen stable bandage. Renew after twenty-four hours.

*Fomentation.* This is a useful treatment for pain or swelling (septic wounds, sprains, contusions). Take a clean square of blanket or towelling 24 × 30 in (610 × 762 mm), fold it into four and hold two of the corners. Place it in a bucket of warm water to which salt has been added (two handfuls of salt to the bucket), then wrap the 'pad' round the injured area. Re-immerse and re-apply, keeping the temperature of the water constant, for about twenty minutes. The treatment can be repeated two or three times a day.

Far left: A saddlery auction is a very good way to buy reasonably priced tack but great care must be taken to check its condition. Left: Harness making is one of Man's oldest crafts, and is now an important industry in Britain, Europe, America and Australia. As much of the equipment used for horses is still made by hand, it is expensive to buy. It is important, therefore, to care for it well so that it does not need to be renewed too often.

*Tubbing.* This is for use with all injuries of the lower leg or feet. Half-fill a wooden bucket (rubber or plastic buckets can be used but never metal buckets or tin feed bins), with a salt-and-warm-water mixture. Pick out the foot and thoroughly clean it, using a second bucket. Place the foot gently into the wooden bucket. Splash the water up the limb with the hand, keeping the temperature of the water constant. Continue this for twenty minutes. Repeat twice daily in cases of severe injury.

*Hose-piping.* This is a very old and effective method for treating a wound or swelling. It is also very good for horses in training after hard work. It should not be carried out in frosty weather and the heels must be packed with vaseline to protect them. Start off by gently 'playing' a hose jet of water on the feet or foot then move up the leg to the knee and forearm muscle. Gradually increase the pressure, continuing for twenty minutes, twice daily if the swelling is large.

*Steaming a head.* This is used for severe colds or nasal catarrh. Put a handful of soft hay in the bottom of a canvas bag, add a teaspoonful of Friars balsam or eucalyptus oil, then pour on a 0.5 pint (0.3 litre) of boiling water. Swing the bag for two minutes, then place it under the horse's muzzle. Allow the horse to inhale for some five minutes, then add more hot water and repeat. The treatment should not be carried out more than twice a week.

*Giving medicine.* A simple and efficient method is to add medicine to the feed, if the horse is not too ill to eat. The powder or mixture should be mixed into a dampened feed. It is advisable to 'starve' the patient for a day, i.e., to miss the morning and mid-day feeds and give the medicated feed in the evening, or give a light feed in the morning, miss the mid-day one, then give the medicated one in the evening. If the medicine will mix easily with water and the horse is not too ill to drink administer it in the drinking water. To

Left: A skewbald mare and foal relax and enjoy the sunshine on a lush, green pasture.
Above: During and after birth, veterinary advice or help must always be sought. If all is well then the mother can be left to rear her foal by herself.

administer an electuary (a stiff paste with treacle), apply the paste to the back of the tongue or the back teeth with a flat piece of wood, which should be some 3.8 mm (1.5 in) in width.

*Drenching*. Raise the head with a rope from the noseband of the head-collar, passed over a beam and held by an assistant. Pour the mixture from a bottle into the side of the mouth. Hold the head up until the drench is swallowed. If the horse coughs or struggles, lower the head and try again. The drenching bottle should be long-necked and the neck must be wrapped with cloth to stop the horse breaking the bottle.

The above are methods used by experienced horsemasters for the treating of minor ailments. Any symptoms or illnesses that you do not understand or cannot recognise should be immediately referred to a veterinary surgeon.